Sticky Note Prayers

How Prayer Spaces in Schools are
Helping to Transform Young Lives

* * *

PHIL SOKELL-MILES

HODDER &
STOUGHTON

First published in Great Britain in 2025 by Hodder Faith
An imprint of John Murray Press

1

Phil Sokell-Miles was formerly known as Phil Togwell.

The poem *The Empty Chair* used with kind permission from Matt Rushby

Photo credits: Tim Abbott, Claire Francis, Lisa Gamble and Phil Sokell-Miles

A CIP catalogue record for this title is available from the British Library

Trade Paperback ISBN 978 1 399 82568 9
ebook ISBN 978 1 399 82569 6

Typeset in Anth by Hewer Text UK Ltd, Edinburgh
Printed and bound in Great Britain by Clays Ltd, Elcograf S.p.A.

John Murray policy is to use papers that are natural, renewable and recyclable products and made from wood grown in sustainable forests. The logging and manufacturing processes are expected to conform to the environmental regulations of the country of origin.

Carmelite House
50 Victoria Embankment
London EC4Y 0DZ

www.hodderfaith.co.uk

John Murray Press, part of Hodder & Stoughton Limited
An Hachette UK company

The authorised representative in the EEA is Hachette Ireland, 8 Castlecourt Centre, Dublin 15, D15 XTP3, Ireland (email: info@hbgi.ie)

Acknowledgements

Tim, in many ways this is your story as well as mine. You hosted many of the early prayer spaces and you were one of the original architects behind so much of what is now multiplying in schools around the world. Thank you for your persistent pioneering, and for your friendship too – this wouldn't have been half as much fun without you.

Rach, I'm fairly certain that this book was your idea, in the sense that you were the first one to say, 'we should write a book about what's happening in prayer spaces in schools.' I think you made this comment back in 2010(!) while we were discussing prayer spaces theology over lunch one day. Thanks for the inspiration, and for being such an important part of this story.

And thanks to everyone else who I've named in this book (whether by real name or by pseudonym). Thank you for sharing your stories with me and for generously giving me permission to retell them here.

There are so many other people who played an important part in the story of Prayer Spaces in Schools, but who aren't named in this book (the early drafts were waaaaay too long!). So thank you Charl, Liz, Joe, Mandy, Tandia, Jeff, Emily, Becky, Ebony, Naomi, Rachel, Jürgen, Susan, Renee, Emma . . . ahh, I knew I shouldn't have started a list. Anyway, you know who you are – this really is *your* story.

And thanks, especially, to all the children and young people who I've met in prayer spaces in schools over the last fifteen years or so - you've taught me so much about prayer. I feel like I understand a little bit more about what Jesus meant when he said, 'if you don't change and become like a child, you will never get into the kingdom of heaven.' (Matthew 18:3, CEV)

Special mention to Ruth, my commissioning editor at Hodder Faith - your enthusiasm for this book is probably one of the reasons that it got published. Thanks to you, and to the rest of the Hodder team for making Sticky Note Prayers a lot better than it was when I first sent it to you. (I think my mum will like her Christmas present this year.)

Finally, Emma, my wife, my best friend. Thank you for believing in me, encouraging me and seeing me through the highs and lows of the writing process, which you probably carried as much as I did. I love you.

Foreword 1

Pete Greig

"These children are at the very centre of life in the kingdom."

– Jesus (Mark 10:14 – MSG)

The legendary footballer Ian Wright played for top teams like Crystal Palace, Arsenal and England. One day he bumped into his old school teacher, Sydney Pigden, after more than thirty years, and immediately broke down in tears. 'Mr Pigden was the first positive male figure in my life', he later explained. Growing up in a Jamaican household in Southeast London, with a father who was absent and a step-father who was abusive, his teacher's faithful, fatherly encouragement had changed his life. It was Syd who taught Ian to read and write, Syd who appointed him to the heady position of 'milk monitor' at school, and Syd who coached him in football.

After leaving school, Ian Wright was caught driving illegally and found himself in prison for 32 days. It was the wake-up call he needed bringing him to his knees

– literally. Late one night in his prison cell he made God a solemn vow: he would sort himself out, live up to Mr Pigden's example, and do whatever it took to succeed as a footballer.

The rest is, as they say, history. Ian Wright would eventually go on to win the Premier League with Arsenal, to lift the European Cup Winners' Cup, and to play for England no fewer than 33 times. He was honoured by the Queen, awarded World Soccer's *Broadcaster of the Year*, and made a Freeman of the City of London. More importantly, he also became a good father to four sons.

The educational environment can undoubtedly make or break kids like Ian Wright. Destinies can be defined, for good or ill, at school. The simple example and encouragement of a good teacher like Syd Pigden, and the positive opportunities healthy schools provide, can set the trajectory of a lifetime.

* * *

I still remember my friend Phil telling me that a local school was planning to turn a classroom into a prayer room. Would it work? Was it actually a sensible idea? But the feedback at the end of that first week left us in little doubt; teachers were delighted and students – even those without religious faith – felt they'd experienced something out of the ordinary. But never in a month of Sundays could we have envisaged what happened next as word spread, the idea caught on, and other schools began establishing their own sacred spaces dedicated to 'cross-curricular, experiential learning'!

Eventually, so many schools made enquiries that Phil came up with the self-explanatory name 'Prayer Spaces in Schools' and began developing resources, building a team, and providing focused leadership.

Phil is far too self-effacing to claim any credit for all of this, and would be the first to point out that the real heroes are teachers and youth workers on the frontline, but without his years of faithful stewardship, Prayer Spaces in Schools could never have become what it is today. Thanks to Phil and his team, countless children and young people, in hundreds of schools across many nations, have been able to process their most heartfelt questions and some of their deepest emotions in a gentle, creative, playful place of Christian prayer. Meanwhile, Phil has looked on like a proud dad as Prayer Spaces in Schools has matured and found its particular place in the world of education and youth provision.

I'm so glad that Phil has finally captured the story of Prayer Spaces in Schools in this book, not just because it's an encouraging testament to a remarkable journey, but also because narratives convey vision and values better than almost anything else.

This is a story worth telling for teachers, youth workers and parents who care about the mental health and spiritual growth of young people today. It'll encourage you but also equip you to take the simple ideas herein and apply them in your own particular context.

This is also a story worth telling because its insights are not just the latest trendy theories – they have been outworked practically and distilled deeply over decades in many different cultural and educational contexts.

Ultimately this is a story worth telling because there are thousands of kids like Ian Wright looking for hope, finding life extraordinarily hard, seeking affirmation, encouragement and meaning beyond the mere mechanics of an academic education. Here we have an opportunity to reach an entire generation in their most formative years and teach them to pray in ways that may shape the rest of their lives.

"Start children off on the way they should go,
and even when they are old they will not turn from it."
Proverbs 22:6

Pete Greig
Waverley Abbey, Lent 2025

Foreword 2

Jodie Avallone

I became a Christian in 2023 and my first prayer space was in December of that same year. I had a lot of questions when I was asked to join the team of volunteers. I felt a sense of panic and unworthiness . . . *why me*? I am shy by nature and I've always been uncomfortable in social situations. And I honestly didn't think that I had any gifts, or that I could be useful to help the children in any way. But despite all this, I offered my feelings to God and I approached the lead-up to the launch of the prayer space with a feeling of excitement.

When I helped to set up the prayer space, I was taken aback by how much effort had gone into the preparation. And somehow, just by being present in the tranquility of the prayer space, God made me aware of a gift of creativity that had been in me since a young age but I hadn't used for a very long time. I also realised that, by joining in as a volunteer, this was giving me the chance to meet and serve alongside people I would never have crossed paths with. I am grateful now for the beautiful and long-lasting friendships that I have formed with many of the other prayer space volunteers.

The thing that impacted me the most though was that I underestimated the power that these prayer spaces can have. I will always remember the faces of the children when they entered the prayer space for the first time. It is a persistent image that I hold close. Clarity and grace filled their eyes. I could see God in each of them.

In a prayer space the atmosphere seems lighter, the noise of the world is non-existent and minds are opened. Our daily lives are too rushed and our minds are too chaotic – it feels like we're never able to deal with anything because of the noise on the outside and within us. And we all – me included – never stop to think that the children around us are also suffering with these noises. Prayer spaces in schools are like medicine for these ongoing problems.

In a prayer space you can just sit with God and concentrate on what's important. You can be at one with yourself and realise who you truly are as an individual, and you can place your worries before God, whether they're physical, mental, emotional or spiritual. And then you leave lighter and a little freer. Not only did I see children set free from worries in the prayer space, but I was too!

I think that prayer spaces are vital, and they should be in every school around the world. For children, they are a safety net. It's the openness. A prayer space allows children to have a voice, and to be heard. It's like a sanctuary. And for me, the prayer space has been a place of realisation, a fresh start – a place that I can only wish heaven is like.

Jodie Avallone

Contents

Acknowledgements v

Foreword 1, by Pete Greig vii

Foreword 2, by Jodie Avallone ix

Part 1: An Introduction . . . Prayer Spaces in Schools

Introduction 3

1. The Tale of Four Prayer Spaces 17
2. Turning the Tide 43
3. Isi . . . and the Rest of the World 69

Part 2: An Explanation . . . the Ministry of Reconciliation

4. Tea with the Professor 99
5. Fearfully and Wonderfully Made 117
6. Let Us Love One Another 145

7. Acting Justly, Loving Mercy, Walking Humbly 171
8. Seeking and Finding 199

Part 3: An Invitation . . . Come On!

9. How to Create Great Prayer Activities 233
10. Just Getting Started 251

Notes 265

Jesus said to them, 'Let the children come to me.'

—Mark 10:14, NLT

Part 1

An Introduction . . .
Prayer Spaces in Schools

I've chopped this book into three parts (this wasn't my idea - one of my early readers suggested it – but I really like it because it helps with the overall flow of the book). The three parts are titled; 'An Introduction . . .', 'An Explanation . . .' and 'An Invitation . . .'

In this first part, I've included stories from some of the early prayer spaces in schools, both in the UK and in other nations too. I've also told the story of my first experience of a prayer space, which took place in my eldest daughter's school. It was a week that I'll never forget, and it changed the course of my life, as you're about to find out.

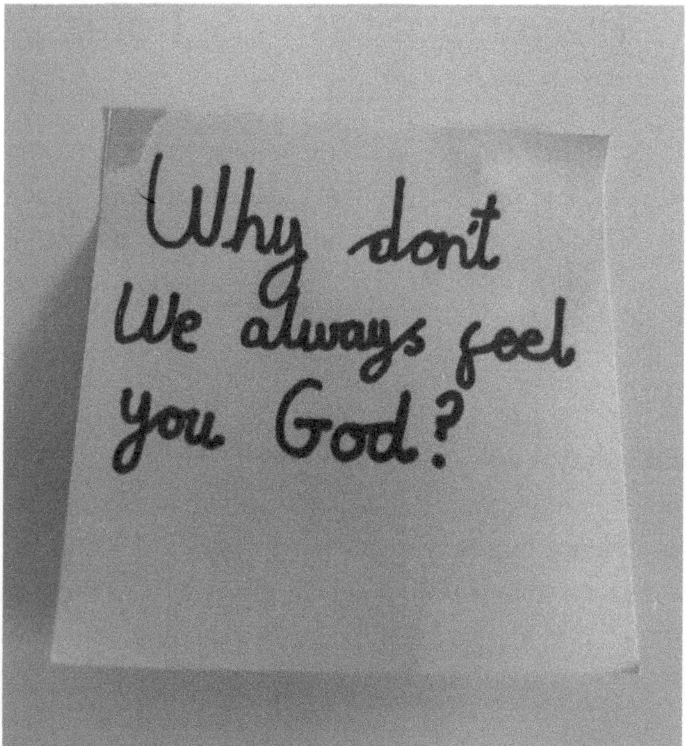
Why don't
We always feel
you God?

Introduction

What pupils say: *'I feel grat wene I am in the preroom, I am aliv!'*—Pupil, aged eight

What education professionals say: *'Every teacher knows that the well being of children is a key issue. We are in a crisis and we have to do something. That is why I think there is a greater openness to spirituality.'*—Education consultant, UK

Let's Imagine . . .

Let's begin by imagining a classroom. We could choose one from almost any kind of school – primary, secondary, inner-city, rural, public, private, church, state/community, or any etcetera you care to add, because there have been prayer spaces in all these types of schools over the last few years – but let's begin with a secondary (or high) school.

The classroom looks a little different from usual. The desks and chairs have been rearranged; some have been removed completely, while others have been pushed together to form six or seven activity islands. On each of the islands there are different objects – a pile of stones, a decorated shoebox with a hole cut in it, some local newspapers, pots of playdough, broken vitamin C tablets in a saucer alongside a large vase of water, a stack of coloured paper with the words 'Letter from God' written across the top of each – and beside most of these objects there are pens, coloured pencils and sticky notes. In one corner of the room there's a small tent. Inside it there are cushions surrounding a five-foot-high vertical tube filled with bubbling water. There's a big old armchair in another corner with some luggage tags and pens on the seat cushion. Beside each of the activities are a couple of laminated sheets of A4 paper, one with a title, like Letting Go, Be Still, The Empty Chair or Prayer Wall, and the other with some simple instructions. To enhance the atmosphere, the sterile fluorescent lights have been switched off, and instead the room is lit with carefully placed bedside lamps and lots of Christmas tree lights. It looks magical.

When the first group of twelve-year-old pupils enters the classroom, there's a bit of confusion and a lot of curiosity. The noisy corridor conversations die down almost immediately, to be replaced with 'What's going on?' and plenty of 'oohs' and 'ahhs'. The members of the small team who arrived earlier to set up the prayer space are dotted around the room, and the team leader welcomes the class and invites them to sit on a large rug in the middle. She asks them what they imagined it would be like when they knew they were coming to 'a prayer space'. One of the boys immediately responds, 'Something boring!' He's the class joker, of course, and he gets a laugh. 'Rows of chairs,' adds someone else. 'Something religious, with Bibles and a big cross.' Another ripple of laughter. 'I didn't expect this,' says one of the girls. 'I thought we'd have to be quiet and close our eyes and stuff, but this is different.' The pupils already seem more interested than they were a few moments ago.

The leader briefly introduces the four others on her team and explains that they are all Christians from a couple of local churches. 'Don't worry, I'm not going to talk for long,' she promises. 'We want you to have plenty of time to explore the prayer space, but before you get started, I want you to understand a few important things.' She looks around the room, trying to catch the attention of as many of the pupils as possible. 'Some of you probably have a religious faith of some sort,' she says. 'Maybe it's a faith that you've chosen for yourself, or maybe it's a faith that you've inherited from your family. If that's you, we hope that the activities we've set up will help you to reflect on some of what your faith means to you and how it works for you. In particular, we hope that this experience will help you to explore how to pray in simple, creative ways.

'Others of you probably wouldn't say that you have a religious faith – you wouldn't call yourself a Christian or a Muslim or a Hindu or whatever – but you do believe that there's something more to life than what we can see and hear and touch. In fact, if the researchers are right, the majority of you in this room feel like this. Some of you might describe this as being spiritual or soulful, but whatever you call it, this prayer space is for you too. We're confident that the activities in this room will help you to reflect on some of what you think and feel about yourself, about other people, about the world that we all live in together and about that "something more to life" stuff too.

'But there may be a few of you who don't believe in any of this religious or spiritual stuff, and if that's you, you're also very welcome.' She smiles reassuringly. 'Please don't be put off by the fact that we've called this a prayer space. Other schools sometimes call theirs soul spaces or reflection spaces if that's any help to you? Look,' she says as she points to the shoebox with the hole cut in it, 'that activity is about letting go of worries. And over there we've got one called Big Questions.' She points to a portable clothes rail with pieces of string hanging from it. '*Everyone* worries about things sometimes, and *everyone* has big questions about things – about life, the universe, suffering, relationships, even God – don't they? And over there we've got an activity about being sorry – everyone has to say sorry sometimes too. I'm guessing that even your teacher has to say sorry sometimes . . . don't you?' The team leader turns to the surprised teacher, who smiles awkwardly and nods, to the amusement of some of the pupils. 'My point is this . . . these activities aren't just for people with religious faith like me, or even for those with spiritual beliefs. They're for . . . human beings! They're essentially about becoming better human beings. So, as long as we're all human beings . . .' She pauses and smiles, glancing around the room as if to check, and is met by more smiles in return – everyone seems to be feeling more relaxed now. 'Yep, I think we're all human beings here today, and so we – all of you – are welcome. The activities in this prayer space have been created to help you explore what it means to be more fully human . . . more kind, more forgiving, more hopeful, more confident, more connected with others, more curious, more engaged in the world that we all live in together, etcetera. All of this is for all of you to use in a way that is meaningful for you.

'And one final thing,' she adds, as if it's an afterthought. 'There may, of course, be one or two of you who just don't want to be here at all – maybe you wish you'd gone to a geography lesson instead?' More laughter, even from the teacher now. 'If that's you, I'm sorry, but this is your lesson time and so you have to stay. Having said that, if you don't want to do any of the activities, you don't have to. There won't be a test at the end and you won't be marked on your participation. All we ask is that you don't spoil it for others, OK? If you want to just wander around and have a look at the activities, you can do that. Just don't interrupt those who want to use them, because the next thirty minutes are going to be really, really important for some of your friends. And who knows, maybe you'll find something that interests you, and the next thirty minutes may prove to be important for you too.

'Has anyone got any questions?' she asks. And there are none, of course, because everyone in the class now feels invited to come as they are. They feel safe to be themselves and they're keen to get started. And so they do . . . on their own, in pairs, in groups of friends. For the next thirty minutes they explore the prayer activities, while the team offers encouragement and support where it's needed.

Just before the end of the lesson, the team leader invites the pupils to finish what they're doing and come back to the rug in the centre of the room. She asks them some questions about their experience of the prayer space. What activities did they like, and why? What ones didn't they like so much, or maybe there were some they found more difficult? Do they feel any different from when they first arrived? Has this experience affected what they think or feel about prayer? The teacher is a bit surprised when hands immediately go up. The pupils seem eager to talk, which hasn't been his experience of this particular class. One boy talks about feeling peaceful, and there's a murmur of agreement around the room. Another talks about letting go of something important when he used the Forgiveness Stones activity. A girl smiles at the friend sitting next to her as she explains that they've been arguing a lot recently, but the Reconciliation Zips activity helped them to sort things out. A boy says that he's never really believed in God, but now he's not so sure. The atmosphere in the room is completely different from thirty minutes ago, and everyone seems to feel it. When the bell rings to mark the end of the lesson, some of the pupils seem reluctant to leave.

For those who have already organised and hosted prayer spaces in schools, this will seem very familiar. It won't require much for you to picture this classroom and imagine these responses, because you've seen them and heard others like them, over and over again. And you will have plenty of your own stories – hundreds of them, I expect.

At the time of writing, there have been at least 7000 prayer spaces in schools in more than thirty-five different nations. And these are just the ones that we've tracked and supported – the ones that we are absolutely certain have taken place. We're pretty sure that there have been hundreds, maybe thousands, more than this, because thousands of people have participated in Prayer Spaces in Schools training sessions over the years, and tens of thousands of resources have been downloaded from our websites. So when we say that a million children and young people have participated in a prayer space in their school, that's just a conservative estimate too . . . and we can only imagine how many of these children and young people have used the opportunity to try praying for the very first time in their lives.

I love these numbers. But I love the stories of children and young people being transformed – even just a little bit – by the presence of Jesus in their school even more (which is why you'll find lots of stories in this book). And it's worth remembering that right now, somewhere around the world, there are almost certainly children and young people in a prayer space in their school. So, before we go any further, how about we pause for a moment and pray specifically for them?

P.R.A.Y.

We pray for every child and young person who will visit a prayer space in their school today.
Help them to PAUSE and be still. May they know that you are with them, God.
Help them to REFLECT, to be honest and open with themselves, and with you too.
Help them to find a way to ASK you for whatever they need today.
And help them to YIELD, to say YES to your invitation to them, 'Come, follow me today.'[1]

How to Use this Book

Before you really get started with this book, there are a couple of things I'd like to say. The first is that although I often get introduced as the person who started Prayer Spaces in Schools, it's not entirely true. The story of Prayer Spaces in Schools is the coming together of lots of people's stories, some of which I have attempted to tell in this small book. My only regret is that we don't have the space to tell *every* story from *every* prayer space, because they all feel important to me, and they all contribute in some way to a Much Bigger Story of what Jesus is doing in the lives of children and young people in schools around the world.

The second thing is that I've tried to make a lot of space for the voices and the experiences of children and young people in this book. One of the chapters, for example, is mostly devoted to conversations with the fourteen-year-old girl who organised the first prayer space in a school in Germany. Unless I have been given specific permission to do otherwise, I have changed names in order to preserve the anonymity of the children and young people (and some of the adults) who feature in these pages.

And finally, while I've included examples of prayer activities in the chapters that follow, you can find literally hundreds more via the Prayer Spaces in Schools websites, which also contain 'How To Get Started' guides, video resources and lots of stories and case studies from prayer spaces in schools just like yours. We've tried to fill these websites, and our social media channels (just do an online search for 'prayer spaces in schools'), with all the information that you could possibly need to get started.

So, whether you're holding this book because you're vaguely interested in prayer spaces in schools, or because someone gave it to you thinking that you might be, or because you're already involved in hosting them, I hope you'll feel encouraged by what you're about to read. And if you're not already involved in hosting prayer spaces, I'm also praying that you'll feel inspired to join in somehow. The need for prayer spaces in schools has never been greater.

* * *

Towards the end of each chapter, I've included a few questions or suggestions for reflection and prayer, based on the content of that chapter. Here are three to get you started:

Reflect and Pray

1. If you've never seen what a prayer space in school looks like, why don't you stick a bookmark in this page and quickly check out one of the Prayer Spaces in Schools websites or social media channels to look at a few of the photos and videos.

2. Think of a couple of children or young people you personally know who are at school – maybe they're at school right now – and quickly ask God to be with them today, for God to protect them and strengthen them. How about praying for them every day until you finish this book? Maybe it'll become a habit that you continue long after you've finished.

3. Ask God to speak to you as you read this book, and maybe pray Isaiah's simple, dangerous prayer: *'God, here am I. Send me!'*[2]

PRAYER ACTIVITY: PRAYER WALL

At the end of each chapter, I've included an example of a prayer activity that is often used in prayer spaces in schools. I mentioned the Prayer Wall in my description of an imaginary prayer space above, and it's a really simple idea, so let's start with that.

What is it?

This activity provides an open space for pupils to write or draw their thoughts or prayers and add them onto their own Prayer Wall.

How does it work?

All you need is a large flat space such as a notice board or sheets of paper hung on a wall or a window, together with some sticky notes and some pens. Make sure the wall is accessible and put the sticky notes and pens nearby. If you are working with younger children you will need to consider their height too. Invite pupils to write or draw their thoughts or their prayers onto sticky notes and then stick them onto the Prayer Wall.

Who is it for?

This prayer activity will work with any age group.

Any other information?

Once this gets going, it won't need any introduction or explanation. After each session ask your team to check all the new sticky notes and remove anything inappropriate. One way to check quickly is to mark each note that you've read with a small dot in one corner.

Instructions

In Jerusalem there is a wall called the Western Wall where people have posted their thoughts and prayers – the outpourings of their hearts – to God for 2000 years. This is like our Prayer Wall. If you want to, you can write or draw a thought or a prayer on a sticky note and stick it onto the Prayer Wall.

A little story . . .

Dan was speaking to a group of church leaders when he showed them a slide of a Prayer Wall covered in sticky notes. One of the leaders stuck up his hand. 'But what do you do with all the prayer requests?' he asked. Dan was confused. 'What do you mean? What prayer requests?' 'The ones that the children write onto the sticky notes,' he said, pointing at the screen. Dan suddenly realised what the church leader meant. 'Oh, by all means, you can pray afterwards for the children who wrote these notes, that's great,' said Dan, 'but they aren't prayer *requests* . . . they're prayers.'

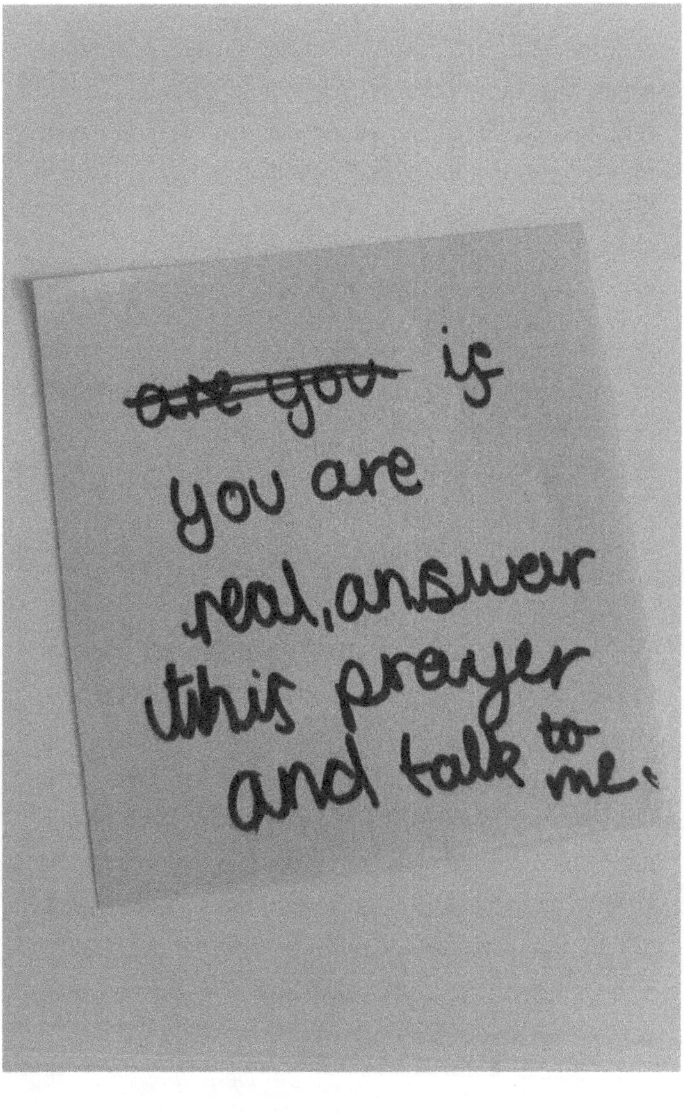
is
you are
real, answer
this prayer
and talk to me.

1

The Tale of Four Prayer Spaces

What pupils say: *'I really enjoyed this, it made me cry with happiness. I am very grateful and I wish I could experience it more often. I would recommend this to other people.'*—Pupil, aged thirteen

What teachers say: *'I spent two hours close to tears as the pupils' responses took my breath away. I knew that they would enjoy being somewhere different and doing something unusual. What I wasn't prepared for was the depth with which they would engage with the prayer space.'*—Head of religious education, UK

Beginnings

Beginnings are important. We all like a good origin story, and this chapter is my best attempt at one for Prayer Spaces in Schools. Think of it as a flashback scene from a movie – the scene that tells you where it all began. Kind of.

I say 'kind of' because prayer spaces actually popped up in a few different places within a few short months of each other, organised by people who had no idea that others were doing something almost identical elsewhere. (Coincidence or God-incidence? I know what I think!) And so what you're about to read are the stories of the first four prayer spaces in schools (although there may, of course, have been others).

Chichester, West Sussex, UK

The first beginning was in Chichester, a pretty cathedral city on the south coast of England, and the birthplace of the 24–7 Prayer movement, of which Prayer Spaces in Schools is a part.

The 24–7 Prayer movement began in a warehouse on an industrial estate just off the ring road that encircles Chichester. The building wasn't easy to find, and even when my wife, Emma, and I pulled into the car park we weren't entirely sure we'd come to the right place. Until we went through the door, that is.

This was October 1999, just a few weeks after the team at Revelation Church in Chichester had launched their 24–7 Prayer Room on 5 September. Pete Greig, one of the church leaders, had called me and suggested that we come for a visit, so the following weekend we bundled as many young people as we could into a couple of cars and drove the ninety or so miles from where we lived in Romford, just east of London. I still remember the sensory overload as I opened the door of that first 24–7 Prayer Room: the background sounds of ambient drum-and-bass worship music and people quietly praying; the chaos of colour on every surface of the room – boldly graffitied prayers of gratitude, cries of lament, words and images . . . and as for the smell! It wasn't just the smell emanating from students who'd spent a little too long in a badly ventilated room though. You'll have to forgive the cliché because I can't think of a better way to describe it, but it felt like there was *another fragrance* in the room. It was something that we would soon come to recognise in 24–7 Prayer Rooms all over the world – the incense of the prayers of the people of God.[1]

To my surprise, the teenagers we'd brought along got stuck in immediately, grabbing paint and Bibles and finding new ways to express what they wanted to say to God. Leaving them to it, I went outside and sat on the front steps with Pete and listened as he told stories about what had happened during those first few weeks. He talked about young people returning to the Prayer Room again and again, some staying for hours on end. He talked about young people praying for the first time, and about others becoming Christians. (For more about the start of the 24–7 Prayer movement, read Pete's extraordinary book *Red Moon Rising*.)[2] At the time, Pete and the team were beginning to wonder what was stirring and spreading, having already filled more than a month with non-stop prayer. But if you'd told him back then that this simple, creative 24–7 Prayer Room would spark a movement that would continue for more than twenty-five years (with no sign of slowing down), and that it would spread into more than half the nations on earth, I suspect Pete would have laughed.

One of the students who prayed in that first 24–7 prayer room was eighteen-year-old Carla. It was a new experience for her, as was the city, where she'd recently arrived for her first year as a student, but both quickly became home. After a few months, Carla offered to volunteer some of her time to help support and resource the other 24–7 Prayer Rooms that were popping up around the UK, and in other nations too. Eventually, this turned into an actual job, and Carla became one of 24–7 Prayer's first employees.

Fast-forward nine years to April 2008, when Carla received an unexpected email from the head of the religious education (RE) department at a local secondary school: she knew about the prayer rooms that Revelation Church had been hosting over the last eight to nine years, and she wanted to know if the church could help set up something similar in one of the school classrooms as part of a special day for the Year 10 cohort (fourteen- to fifteen-year-olds). 24–7 Prayer Rooms had already been escaping church buildings and popping up in some unusual places – shopfronts in town centres, youth clubs, nightclubs, even the Houses of Parliament in London – but a school? This was something brand new. Nevertheless, Carla emailed an enthusiastic reply: 'Yes, of course!'

Three months later, in July 2008, a team from Revelation Church transformed one of the carpeted classrooms into a prayer space. They blacked out the windows and used rope-lights and lamps to illuminate the room. They hung sheets to break up the space, and suspended a huge net filled with coloured balloons in the centre of the room. There were cushions and mirrors, sticky notes and pens, cardboard boxes to crawl into and a huge wooden cross to pin 'help me' prayers onto. It looked amazing.

'I remember being surprised at the pupils' honesty,' said Carla afterwards. 'Small classes of fourteen- to fifteen-year-old pupils were timetabled to visit the prayer space throughout the day, and I thought that maybe the odd one would pray. I really didn't expect them all to interact, but they did. When I read what they wrote on the sticky notes, I was surprised, and then when I read the feedback book, I was deeply moved. The pupils wrote about stress and anxiety, about the prayer space being a peaceful place. One even wrote: "Wow, please can we have this all the time?"'

A few months later, the head of RE emailed again to ask Carla if the team could host another prayer space, but this time as part of the school's arts festival. She wanted something that would stimulate spiritual reflection, and she couldn't think of anything better. This time the prayer space was open for longer, for more pupils, and it was outside, too. They even parked a small '24–7 Prayer' caravan on the school playground as a mobile prayer space. Something was stirring.

Ryton, Tyne and Wear, UK

The next beginning happened 350 miles from Chichester (which is about the furthest you can get from Chichester and still be in England) in an ex-coal mining village in Tyne and Wear called Ryton. About a year before Carla and the team from Revelation Church opened their first prayer space, a Church of England vicar in Ryton was putting the finishing touches to the plans for his first 24–7 Prayer week.

The Reverend Tom Jamieson was excited, but he was nervous too, because his ageing Anglican community had never done anything like this before. They'd joined forces with three of the other denominational churches in their small village of 8500 people to host the 24–7 Prayer Room together, because, in Tom's own words, 'We were all pretty traditional, none with significant numbers of youth or young adults, and we were all deeply concerned about that and not sure what to do.'

They chose the United Reformed Church (URC) hall for their 24–7 Prayer Room and added a few other things to welcome visitors. Just inside the main doors, they turned the tired kitchen area into a coffee shop, which they opened from 7 a.m. until 9 p.m. throughout the week. In some of the side rooms they set up creative arts and crafts, and there was a reading room too. And then, right at the back of the building, in the large living room with a huge bay window that overlooked an overgrown garden, they set up the Prayer Room. Tom and his team of volunteers printed invitations and gave them out to everyone in the community, including the head teacher at the local secondary school, which was just a stone's throw from the URC hall.

It's not unusual for local church ministers in the UK to still do short talks in school assemblies, and Tom had been doing this kind of thing for a while. So he asked if he could do a talk during some of the assemblies for each of the year groups about the Prayer Room, and when the head teacher said yes, Tom was delighted, but also a bit nervous about what the pupils would make of it.

Two weeks later, Tom stood in front of 200 sixth-form (seventeen- and eighteen-year-old) pupils. He told them a story about a friend who'd recently visited the Isle of Skye in Scotland because he needed space to think clearly about his life. 'We all need space like this from time to time, don't we?' he asked as he looked around at the sea of faces. He sensed that they agreed. 'So,' Tom took a deep breath and continued, 'the Ryton churches have set up a special space for the town. It's a new endeavour for us, but lots of churches up and down the country have been doing this kind of thing for a while now – people call them 24–7 Prayer Rooms – and we'd like to invite you to visit ours.' At the end of the assembly Tom handed out some of the invitations that he'd printed, which included directions to the hall next door and the times when it would be open outside school hours, silently praying for each pupil as he did so.

'We invited a few people,' said Tom afterwards, 'but in the end it was children and young people who were doing most of the inviting. Children from the local primary school came with their parents and siblings. Christian pupils from the secondary school brought their friends during lunch breaks, and then those friends brought other friends. On Friday the head teacher's personal assistant dropped in because, as she said, "Pupils are telling staff that they mustn't miss the Prayer Room so I thought I'd better come."

'A religious education class came to the Prayer Room early in the week. They told me that their next class that day, I think it was history, had been abandoned by the teacher (she was a Christian) on account of the number of pupils who were in tears when she arrived. She decided to just let them talk about what they had experienced; history could wait another day!

'I remember one boy in particular,' Tom continued. 'His class had visited the Prayer Room, and I'd gathered them together at the end of their lesson for some feedback. He described one of the prayer activities that he had been using and he wept openly as he tried to talk about it. What struck me was that this boy clearly felt safe with us in the Prayer Room, and also the empathy and support that he received from his classmates.' Tom's own eyes were wet with tears as he told this story.

On Friday lunchtime, the final day, Tom had arranged to meet a fourteen-year-old girl, one of the pupils and a leader among the teenage members of the local Methodist Church, to ask what her friends had thought and felt about the week. Tom gently pushed the door of the Prayer Room open, only to find a pile of shoes in the entrance. As the week had progressed, pupils had been taking off their shoes before entering the Prayer Room, but he wasn't expecting to find this many. Peering round the door, he saw the girl sitting on the floor in the middle of the room, surrounded by a group of her friends, confidently answering their questions. 'So, how do I pray?' one asked. 'You said that God speaks to you – how does God do that? How can you hear God?' asked another. 'How do I become a Christian?'

Tom eased himself back out and closed the door as

quietly as he could. When he got outside, he called me and told me what had been going on. 'In the weeks before our 24–7 Prayer week, we asked God to touch the hearts of young people,' he told me. 'God has done so with an abundance of love and grace. The question is, do we go back to church as normal after this?'

Farnham, Surrey, UK

Our third beginning took place in between Chichester and Ryton, in a leafy market town called Farnham, just south of London. When Jane Whittington started her role as the head teacher of one of Farnham's primary schools, the school was in what's known as 'special measures', which means that it had fallen below the government's standards. She knew that this was going to be a challenge, but she'd recently been inspired by a book written by another head teacher who'd taken on a failing school in London.[3] In it, the author talked about putting the spiritual heart back into a school, and Jane knew that this was exactly what she wanted to do.

During Jane's first year, a group of local Christians had been helping to lead some assemblies and lessons. When they asked what more they could do, Jane replied, 'I want my pupils to experience prayer. I want them to understand that prayer is more than just hands-together and eyes-closed.' When I asked her why she'd made this a priority, she told me that she'd started praying with two friends back in 1984, in the build-up to the American evangelist Billy Graham's stadium crusade called Mission England. 'And we're still praying!' she said with a smile. 'Prayer has always been an important part of my life, and I wanted my pupils to discover that they could pray about anything, anywhere, in the same way that I'd learnt.'

One of this group of local Christians had some experience of '24–7 Prayer stuff', so they borrowed ideas from that and developed a plan for a prayer space. Jane loved what they were proposing, but realised that there wasn't any room for it in the school building, so they decided to pitch a tent on the school field instead. Inside the tent they marked out four zones labelled 'Please', 'Thank You', 'Sorry' and 'Wow!', and they created a couple of prayer activities to go in each zone for the children to use.

The prayer space in Farnham launched in May 2008. The local Christians hosted an assembly for the whole school and invited the pupils to come and visit the prayer space. The pupils seemed keen, but no one expected the queue that stretched right around the field during the very first lunch break. One of the children in the queue was a ten-year-old boy whose behaviour in school was sometimes a bit challenging. Jane wasn't sure if he would be interested, but to her surprise he loved the prayer activities. 'That was awesome!' he said as he left the prayer space. Jane reflected afterwards, 'That was the moment I thought that this thing might just work.'

Almost every child in the school visited the prayer space voluntarily that week. And Jane took the whole staff team in for one of their meetings too, just so they could experience it for themselves. For some children, especially those who were 'looked after' (meaning they were under the care of the local authority's social services in some way), the prayer space became a haven – a place of safety and belonging.

The local Christians, and Jane herself, learned a lot from their first prayer space experience, and it became a catalyst for all sorts of exciting things over the years that followed. They formed a special prayer space team called Orison (an Anglo-French word meaning 'prayer'), and with an ex-primary school teacher, Rach Warwick, as their team leader, they were among the early pioneers of prayer spaces in schools around England. At Jane's school the Orison team worked with a group of children to create some new prayer activities (such as Hope Blossoms and Jumping For Joy), many of which are still being used in prayer spaces in schools today.

After one of Orison's first prayer spaces in Addleston, not far from Farnham, Rach emailed me to say, 'The pupils really appreciated the space, and seem to have got lots out of it. We interviewed some of the twelve-year-old pupils yesterday morning and one girl said that when she came into the prayer space she felt like she had been "opened". She said the experience had changed her views on prayer and that she wants it to be a part of her life now. We also had several comments from staff about how the prayer space was affecting the rest of the school – teachers commented that pupils were calmer and that breaks and lunchtimes were quieter, with pupils shouting at each other much less.'

Just nine months after Jane arrived in Farnham, her school came out of 'special measures' because of the obvious improvements that had taken place. And six years later, Jane moved into a new role as a member of the education team for the Church of England's Diocese of Guildford, where she championed prayer spaces in schools and hosted regular training events for churches and schools across the region, resulting in dozens more prayer spaces.

Colchester, Essex, UK

The final beginning was in the city of Colchester. Tim Abbott and the Christian Youth Outreach (CYO) team had started talking about the possibility of prayer spaces in schools in the autumn of 2007, around the same time that Tom and the Ryton churches were running theirs. However, CYO didn't actually host its first prayer space until July the following year, the same month as Carla and the Revelation Church team hosted theirs in Chichester, and just a few weeks after Jane's prayer space was launched in Farnham. Even as I write this, I find it extraordinary that, at this stage, none of them knew about any of the others.

I have a certain affection for Colchester because it's where I was born. My family moved when I was very young though, so I wasn't there for long. Tim, on the other hand, has lived there and has served Colchester's churches and its schools for more than thirty years. Colchester has at least fifteen secondary schools (depending on where you draw the geographical line around it), and the CYO team have worked in all of them, delivering lessons, leading Christian unions and lunchtime clubs, appointing chaplains, offering pastoral support during times of bereavement and (of course) hosting prayer spaces.

Tim had already helped to organise a 24–7 Prayer Room for churches across the city in May 2000, less than a year after the very first Prayer Room was set up in Chichester, and then he was involved in opening another one in a public shopfront in 2004. Drawing on these experiences of creative, hospitable reflection and prayer, Tim and his team came up with a proposal for a 'prayer room for pupils'. They decided to send it to the heads of RE and some of the head teachers at four local secondary schools. Not all of these teachers were Christians, but to Tim's astonishment, all four schools said yes.

The CYO team decided to host their first prayer space at a secondary school in the north of Colchester. Having led assemblies, RE lessons and lunchtime groups in this school, they were already well known and warmly welcomed. However, before they could launch their first prayer space, they needed to decide what to call it. 'We wanted to give it a name that we felt pupils would be comfortable using when describing it to their friends,' explains Tim. 'We felt that using the word "prayer" might mean that young people would have preconceived ideas about the room that didn't actually relate to what it offered.'[4] After discussing a few options, the word 'sanctuary' felt like the best fit, although, in Tim's words, 'it felt a bit cumbersome'. But then someone suggested Sanctum, and that's when they knew they'd found their name: Sanctum – a sacred space in schools.

When Sanctum launched, it was open during break times, lunchtimes and then before and after the school day. (At that time, no connection was envisaged with subject lessons.) The CYO team had designed posters and put them up around the school to try and persuade pupils to come and visit, but after a quiet start they decided to head out into the playground during break times to invite pupils personally. By the end of the second day, the pupils who had visited were calling it 'The Jesus Room', and after just four days, more than 100 pupils had experienced Sanctum.

The comments that pupils wrote in the visitors' book offered a few insights into the impact that this simple space of reflection and prayer – and especially the Be Still tent – was having:

'Very relaxing. It was a pleasure to be here and I will come again.'

'This place is amazingly peaceful. I loved it. This was a place where I could let out my true feelings.'

'It was very good, especially the tent because it was very peaceful and it lets you express your feelings to God.'

'I loved being in the tent space. It is such a relaxing and peaceful place. A great way to spend some time in the day. I would like this in my house.'

Over the next twelve months, Tim and the CYO team were invited to run Sanctum in other schools, and in the years since then nearly every secondary school in the city has welcomed a Sanctum prayer space, many making it an annual event.

One of the young people who experienced a Sanctum prayer space was a thirteen-year-old girl called Lauren. Tim wrote the following reflections in his blog:

> Lauren had already done about three prayer activities before sitting down next to Natalie, one of the Sanctum team. To start with all she could say was 'I just feel so overwhelmed. It's all so overwhelming.' The activities obviously had a profound impact on her, especially the ones focusing on 'letting go' and 'forgiveness'.
>
> Later in the lesson Lauren came over to a teacher to explain in breathless wonder what being in the Sanctum prayer space had done for her. It was humbling to hear someone speaking so passionately about such a personal, spiritual revelation, and it's difficult to gauge what Lauren's longer term response will be to her experience. What's abundantly clear though is that her world has been interrupted, her soul impacted and her spirit awakened by something she wasn't expecting, but which has brought wonder and joy to her life. At the end of the lesson, Lauren wrote, 'I really enjoyed this, it made me cry with happiness. I

am very grateful and I wish I could experience it more often. I would recommend this to other people.'

At the time of writing, CYO has hosted more than sixty-five Sanctum prayer spaces, and it estimates that more than 26,000 pupils – young people just like Lauren – have participated in them. Heaven only knows the impact that these prayer spaces have had on these young lives.

Susie's Story

Prayer spaces can sometimes have as big an impact on those who volunteer to be part of the teams as they do on the pupils who visit them. Susie was part of CYO's Sanctum prayer space teams. She worked in a church coffee shop, and Tim had a feeling that she would be great at helping out with a secondary school prayer space, so he asked her. To her surprise, and in spite of her apprehension about working with teenagers, Susie said yes.

After her day in the prayer space Susie emailed Tim:

> Today I went and was part of something so very special I actually didn't want to leave. The pupils were lovely, polite, engaging and interested in what was being offered to them. I would never in a million years have volunteered to

do this but am so glad I went. I found myself challenged, stretched and way out of my comfort zone. I went this morning thinking what on earth can I offer these young people. It turns out, all they needed was my time and for me to be interested in them. That was all.

The First Question

The four prayer spaces I've just described took place in different types of schools (three high schools and one primary school, two church schools and two community/state schools) in different socio-economic areas. They were open at different times and pupils participated in them in different ways, and they were also hosted by very different teams of volunteers. However, one thing stands out as common to all four of these stories, and it's the willingness of Christians to serve the pastoral and spiritual needs of their local school community.

The prayer space planning process doesn't actually begin by choosing a room and downloading prayer-activity resources. It begins with an important question: '*Why* do you want to run a prayer space in your local school?'

I once asked a group of youth workers this question during a training session and one of them told me they were hoping and praying that the church's youth group would double in size. There were six teenagers in his group at that time. When I told him that his vision was too small, I think he was expecting me to simply suggest a bigger number, so he was a bit puzzled when I continued, 'Why not win the whole school community?' I wasn't, of course, suggesting that everyone in the school community would join his church youth group, and I wasn't even suggesting that's what he should hope and pray for. I was trying to encourage him to consider a different missional approach, to recognise that most of the time the mission of God isn't about 'going and bringing back' but about 'going and staying'; it's about going and being, going and serving . . . and seeing what Jesus builds.

So, before we start preparing all the practical stuff for our first (or our 101st) prayer space, let's remember to ask the Holy Spirit to help us prepare our hearts . . . to go and serve, by staying. Go and be a blessing. Go and make friends. Go and give the very best of ourselves. Go and seek first (and by seek, I mean 'partner with the Holy Spirit in bringing about') the kingdom of heaven among the whole school community in every possible creative, life-giving way. Go and help to make the school a kinder, more generous, more joyful, more forgiving, more hopeful, more curious, more loving, more reconciled, more hospitable place to learn and work. Go and become part of it – become an essential part of the school family.

Prayer spaces are fantastic tools, they are catalysts

for all sorts of kingdom of heaven stuff, but they're not the goal. The goal is a great relationship – an ongoing partnership between local Christians and the school community, from which all sorts of good fruit can grow.

* * *

Back in 2008, I was serving as 24–7 Prayer's UK director. One of the best bits about the role was the emails I received. Not *all* of them, of course, but the ones with people's stories from 24–7 Prayer Rooms were always encouraging. When I received the emails about these first four 24–7-style prayer rooms in school classrooms, I wasn't just encouraged though – I was intrigued! Here were four people doing roughly the same thing in schools in four entirely different places around England within a few months of each other . . . and yet *they didn't know each other*. Was this a strange coincidence, or was there something more going on?

According to the writer and philosopher G.K. Chesterton, 'coincidences are spiritual puns'.[5] They're one of God's ways of attracting our attention; they're signs to make us wonder and wander in God's direction. And these four stories definitely got my attention. So I contacted Tim and some of the others who had been involved in those first few prayer spaces and we arranged to meet in 24–7 Prayer's offices in London.

That meeting was a holy moment – I don't know how else to describe it. We listened carefully to each prayer-space story – much longer versions than I've just summarised above. And then we asked questions like: How did your prayer space work? What did the school expect? What did your prayer space look like? What activities did you include? What did the pupils say about their experience, especially those who weren't Christians? What did the *staff* say about the prayer space, especially those who weren't Christians? And crucially: Was your prayer space the result of a unique relationship with the school . . . or is it reproducible?

As I said, it felt holy, conspiratorially so. It felt like we'd been given a sneaky peak at something that God was doing, and it felt like we were being invited to steward seeds that God was planting in a few places where the ground had been prayerfully prepared for a very long time. I have often wondered if this is one of God's favourite ways to work. God gets something started (sometimes barely), and then steps back and beckons for us to join in . . . 'Come and steward this with me! This is going to be so much more fun if we do it together!'

And so we said, 'Yes, Lord', not really knowing what we were saying yes to. And I left the meeting that evening with the overwhelming feeling that I needed to experience one of these prayer spaces in schools for myself.

Reflect and Pray

1. Have you experienced any coincidences lately? Or has anything at home or work or elsewhere caught your attention in an unusual way . . . a conversation, or something you've read or seen on screen? Try this simple prayer from 1 Samuel 3:10 (CEV), 'I'm listening. What do you want me to do?'

2. Do you know a 'Lauren' – someone who isn't a Christian yet, but who has experienced something of the presence of God and is processing what this means and how to respond to it? If so, ask God to speak to them.

3. Tom said about his church, 'We were all pretty traditional, none with significant numbers of youth or young adults, and we were all deeply concerned about that and not sure what to do.' Is your church like Tom's? If so, talk with God about this.

PRAYER ACTIVITY: JUMPING FOR JOY

In honour of all that the Orison team did to pioneer prayer spaces back in those early days, here's one of their prayer activities, Jumping For Joy, which I mentioned in the story of their first prayer space.

What is it?

Joy isn't the same thing as happiness, but it is closely linked. Joy has a lot in common with gratitude because it involves choosing to be positive or to speak positively, even when some things around us are negative. This activity invites pupils to think about the things they feel joyful about and to shout them out.

How does it work?

All you need for this activity is a small exercise trampette/trampoline and some safety mats. Put the trampette onto the safety mat (or some other suitably safe surface). This is a noisy prayer activity, so position it away from activities that require concentration and quiet. Invite pupils to take it in turns to jump/bounce on the trampette and as they jump, to say (or shout!) things that they feel joyful about, things that they are thankful for.

Who is it for?

Unsurprisingly, this activity works best with primary-aged children, and it's probably safer to only use it with them too!

Any other information?

You will need at least one adult supervising this activity to ensure that pupils stay safe.

Instructions

Jump on the trampette. As you jump, think of the things or the people you feel joyful about . . . the things or people you are thankful for. If you want to, say (or shout) them out as you jump.

A little story . . .

Staff at a secondary school in the north of England were invited to visit a prayer space that had been set up for their pupils to use the following week. The first group of teachers who entered the prayer space were a bit puzzled as it clearly wasn't what they were expecting – but after some brief explanations, they started to try out the prayer activities.

A few minutes into the session there was a shriek from one of the school reception staff as she fell off the Jumping For Joy trampette and tumbled onto the floor. As a couple of the other teachers tried to help her up, she howled . . . with laughter! 'Let me go,' she said, brushing them aside and clambering straight back onto the trampette. With a huge grin, she started bouncing again. 'I haven't finished jumping for joy!'

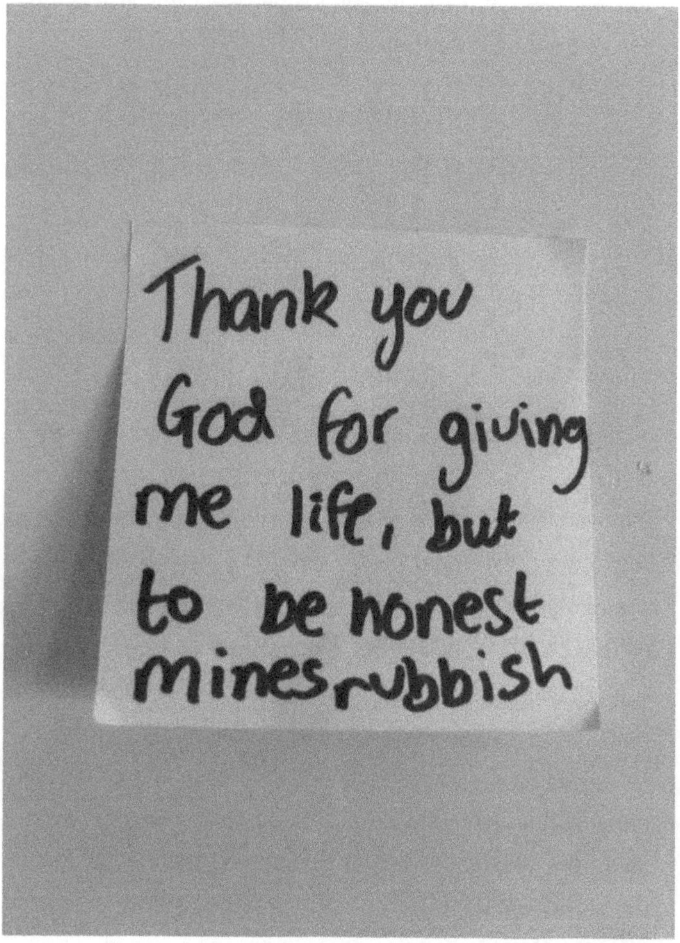
Thank you
God for giving
me life, but
to be honest
mines rubbish

2

Turning the Tide

What pupils say: *'I've never seen prayer displayed or experienced like this before. It's made me realise how many different ways prayer can be appreciated. It's opened up religion into my life again. Thank you!'*—Pupil, aged seventeen

What teachers say: *'I was amazed at how well the pupils engaged with the prayer ideas, and it had a big impact on those of us from the staff team who were there too.'*—Michelle, teacher, UK

God in School

Having heard the stories behind the first four prayer spaces in schools, I really wanted to experience one for myself. Looking back now, I think I *needed* to experience one for myself – to witness God at work in young people's lives – for two very different, but very personal, reasons.

First, I'd been working for 24–7 Prayer for nearly four years by this point, and I was feeling weary. Emma and I were grieving the loss of the church community that we'd left after many years. We were wrestling with the local education system to get the right kind of provision for our middle daughter, who was profoundly deaf. And we were under a lot of pressure financially too. Everything felt difficult. And to be really honest with you, although I knew that God had called me to work with 24–7 Prayer,[1] I was starting to miss my previous jobs.

Since leaving school, I'd worked with young people in all sorts of settings – in youth clubs and nightclubs, at festivals and events, on the streets and in hostels for homeless young people in central London. Helping young people – encouraging and enabling them to live life to the full – felt like what I was made for. Don't get me wrong, I loved serving and working with 24–7 Prayer – every day was, and still is, a privilege – but I was yearning for opportunities to work with young people again. And then, seemingly out of nowhere, I heard these four stories.

For the second reason, I need to rewind even further (a *lot* further). I'm somewhat ashamed to admit this, but when I was at high school, like many Christian teenagers, I lived a bit of a double life. Outside school I did the Christian thing – I went to church, I joined in with the youth group activities and I knew the words of all the songs. Inside school, however, I was just like all my friends – barely anything about the way I talked or behaved suggested that I was following Jesus.

But everything changed when I was around sixteen. I'd just completed my end-of-year exams at school, and it was the start of the long summer break. I'd recently broken up with my first proper girlfriend – I can't remember what went wrong, but I felt devastated at the time. And then a prophetic teacher/preacher from the USA singled me out during a church meeting and said something about it being time to take God's call on my life seriously. I'm sure she meant it to encourage me, but at the time I just felt embarrassed and a little bit angry, probably because I knew that I wasn't taking God's call, nor my life, seriously at all.

A few days later, I was alone in my bedroom and I started praying for the first time in a long while. I told God how I was feeling. I said sorry for a few things that I knew weren't right, and I asked for God's help – specifically, I asked for some new Christian friends at school, because at the time I didn't feel like I had any. In return, I told God that I would try to live differently, try to follow Jesus in school. I didn't have a dramatic, road-to-Damascus experience that day – I definitely didn't hear any voices from heaven or see any visions, and there wasn't any divine writing on my bedroom wall – but as I look back, I recognise it as a turning point in my life.

A couple of months later, I was back at school for the start of my two-year 'A'-level courses. I made some new friends and, to my surprise, some of them were Christians. It seemed like God was honouring our deal, so I tried my best to keep my end of it too. A few weeks later – another surprise! – I got asked to lead the Christian union (CU) along with some of my new friends. We didn't really know what we were supposed to do, so a few of us started meeting before school to pray for one another and for the school. Things began to change almost immediately. We felt more confident talking about Jesus with our classmates. We were given permission to speak about being a Christian during a school assembly, and we hosted discussions about Christianity with the rest of the 'A'-level pupils. We held CU meetings outside during the warmer weather, and we openly offered to pray with those who didn't yet know Jesus. During those two years, we experienced God's presence and witnessed God working in the lives of pupils and teachers in so many ways, and as a result, the CU grew from thirty to around 150 pupils.

All of this was in the back of my mind when I listened to Carla, Tom, Jane and Tim talking about their first prayer spaces. I heard them telling stories of children and young people experiencing God's presence in school classrooms, and I felt something in my spirit awakening: 'Yes! Come on! I know this kind of thing can happen, and I want to see it happen again.' And in order for it to happen, like I said, I needed to experience a prayer space for myself.

My First Prayer Space

Early in July 2008, I was sitting on an uncomfortable moulded-plastic school chair alongside my eleven-year-old daughter. It was enrolment day at her new school and we were waiting in line for our five-minute appointment with her new class tutor.

'Is your name Phil?' said a voice. I looked round and saw a tall, curly haired woman wearing a tracksuit – the universally recognisable uniform of a physical education (PE) teacher – clutching an armful of books and papers. I nodded, slowly.

'My name is Michelle,' she continued, 'and I was hoping I would meet you.' Rummaging through the bundle of papers in her arms, she dug out a battered copy of Pete Greig's book, *Red Moon Rising*.[2] 'I've been reading this book about 24–7 Prayer, and it's given me an idea. Some of my friends told me that you're involved in 24–7 Prayer, and I found out that you were coming this evening, so I've been waiting for you to arrive so I could ask you about my idea . . . Do you think we could set up a 24–7 Prayer Room in our school?'

Less than a week later I was sitting in Michelle's office drinking instant coffee and listening as she told me her extraordinary story. 'I went to a Catholic school, but I didn't really have any faith when I started teaching here,' she admitted. 'However, there were two other teachers who started on the same day as me. One of them was a Christian, and she was always very open about her faith.' Michelle paused and stared at me for a moment. 'In order to understand faith, you need someone to share theirs with you, and she shared hers with me. That's when I became a Christian.

'I started praying for the school,' she said. 'I actually live a forty-five minute drive from here, but I'm glad that I live so far away because it gives me forty-five minutes every day to pray for the pupils.' Michelle then told me that she'd spotted Pete's book about 24–7 Prayer in the local Christian bookshop in Romford. 'I don't honestly know why I picked it up, but I felt like I should read it. I read about prayer rooms in churches and in all sorts of other places, and I began to wonder, could we do a prayer room in one of our classrooms?' I smiled and shook my head in astonishment. 'If you'd asked me that question a few months ago, Michelle, I would've probably said no,' I laughed. 'But let me tell you about four friends of mine . . .'

For the next hour, Michelle and I made plans. The friends who'd told her about me turned out to be Ruth and James, two local Methodist ministers. I called them later that day, and they were keen to help with the prayer space, so the four of us met and talked some more and eventually decided to give it a go.

After a few weeks of planning and preparation, Michelle offered us a small classroom for the week, and

Ruth, James and I spent around four hours attempting to transform it from dull and functional into something a bit more attractive and engaging. We covered the slot-shaped windows and positioned lamps and Christmas-tree lights around the room to help create a bit of atmosphere, and then we removed most of the desks and chairs, keeping just enough for the prayer activities that we'd decided to set up, some of which were based on the ones that Tim and the CYO team had used in Colchester.

On one of the walls, we pinned a large map of the world and surrounded it with printouts of recent news reports. Here, pupils would be invited to write their reflections or prayers onto sticky notes and stick them onto the map. Then we printed out a stack of A5 sheets with the title 'Letter from God' at the top and surrounded these with photos of the school and of the local town centre. Here, pupils would be invited to imagine what God (whether they believed in God or not) might want to say to their school or their town, and then to write it as a short letter.

In one of the corners, we attached a tall mirror to the wall and stuck positive quotes around it from the Bible and from popular culture. To create a little bit of privacy for the pupils while they stood in front of the mirror and read the quotes, we hung a couple of bed sheets from the ceiling. In another corner, we tied more sheets to two pipes that were sticking out of the wall to create a kind of 'tent', which we then filled with bean bags, battery-operated candles and a lava lamp, so that pupils could crawl inside and be still in comfort for a few minutes.

We created a simple Prayer Wall on another wall, and we also set up an activity themed around 'togetherness', which involved glueing broken pieces of tile together to form a large mosaic. This activity didn't really work the way we'd intended, so we removed it after a couple of days (see Chapter 9 for tips on how to create great prayer activities, and how to avoid creating unworkable and/or dangerous ones).

Michelle had talked with the head teacher and they'd agreed that classes wouldn't be brought to the prayer space during lesson times, but that pupils could visit it voluntarily during lunch and break times. Ruth, James and I worked hard to publicise the prayer space by putting posters up around the school proclaiming, 'Come and Check Out the Prayer Space!' and then doing a couple of awkward assembly talks, where we tried to explain what the prayer space would be like, even though we didn't really know ourselves.

And so there we were, in the room, just before the start of the Monday lunch break. Ruth, James and I looked at each other, wondering what was going to happen. I confess, I was sceptical. I wasn't convinced that anyone was going to turn up, and for a short while after the buzzer sounded for lunchtime it looked like I was right.

But then the door opened and a small group of girls peered in. 'Is this the . . . WOH!' one of them said, her eyes wide with surprise. 'This is cool!' They dropped their bags behind the classroom door and Ruth ushered them in and started explaining the Prayer Wall activity. Almost immediately behind them, another group wandered in and reacted in exactly the same way. I asked them to shove their bags under one of the tables and then steered them towards a different prayer activity, while James welcomed yet another group who'd arrived shortly after. Pretty soon, the room was crammed full. While the pupils shuffled slowly from one activity to another, talking, laughing and eating their packed lunches, we did our best to offer a bit of encouragement.

By the time we were halfway through the lunch break, the room was so full of pupils that I was pressed against one of the walls, barely able to move. A teacher poked her head through the open doorway and half-shouted across to me, 'It doesn't seem like there's much praying going on in here?' I shrugged in response. I honestly didn't know what was going on – it felt like we were supervising an overcrowded youth club session rather than hosting a prayer space. Eventually, the buzzer signalled the end of lunchtime and the pupils grabbed their bags and jackets from wherever they'd stashed them, and bundled out of the room. Ruth, James and I breathed a sigh of relief and decided to tidy up a bit before pausing to discuss our first experience. We started replacing pen lids, unsticking plasticine from the floor and repairing our makeshift Be Still tent, which had already collapsed. As I crouched down to pick up the first of dozens of sticky notes that had fallen off the walls, I read something that broke my heart and changed my life.

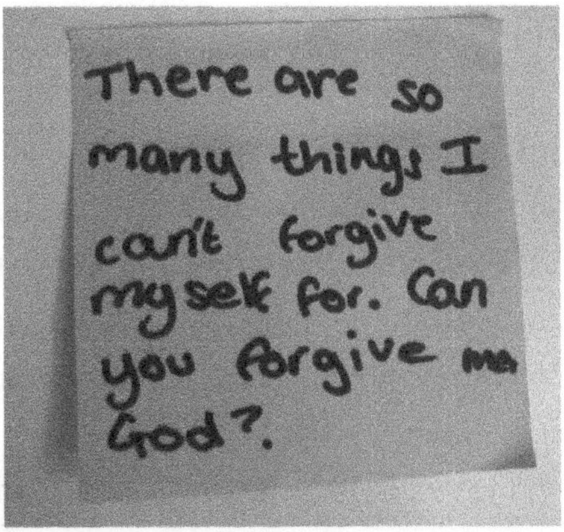

For a moment, I couldn't move. I didn't know what to do. I felt I was holding something sacred, and it didn't seem right to just stick it back onto the wall (with some adhesive putty this time, to keep it there), but then I noticed some of the other sticky notes and realised that they were all just as precious as the one I was holding.

- *'I have no friends.'*
- *'I don't know what is going on. I can't help but cry.'*
- *'Thank you. That's all that I can say . . . this sticky note is too small to list all my thank yous for this place. X'*

We all experience turning points in our lives, moments that really matter, and this was definitely one of mine. This was the moment when I just knew that we needed to offer prayer spaces like this to as many children and young people as we possibly could. They *needed* spaces like this.

It's worth remembering that there weren't any private corners in this prayer space. Pupils were choosing to write their raw, honest, heart-breaking reflections and prayers in front of their friends. The struggles, the hopes and fears, the confusion in their lives – they were so close to the surface that all it took were some simple activities in a safe space, with some safe people, and an invitation . . . to 'try praying, if you want to'. I don't know who wrote the sticky note I picked up off the floor during that lunch break, but I hope that she heard heaven's response, because I'm 100 per cent sure it was something like, 'YES, I do forgive you! I have already! I love you!'

Pupils filled the room during every break time that week. There were 'first timers' every day, of course, but many of the pupils came back over and over again, either to try prayer activities that they'd previously missed, or to talk with one of us about something, and others seemed to just want to be in the room. The Be Still activity was more popular than we expected. Pupils queued to crawl inside our poorly constructed tent to chill out for a few minutes. James was looking after it, and he started restricting pupils to three-minute slots so that everyone got a turn. He joked that it was like looking after an inflatable castle, because he was continually having to get a few pupils out before the next lot could have a go. For the rest of the week, the nickname stuck – Be Still became affectionately known as the Bouncy Castle.

The Mirrors activity – we called it Be Yourself – had a big impact on a lot of the pupils. One girl was in tears as she stood in front of the mirror. 'It isn't like me to cry,' she said to Ruth. 'What's happening?' Later in the week, one of the pupils – a seventeen-year-old girl – visited the prayer space on her own during a study period and asked if she could have a look around while it was quiet. James had gone to find coffee, and Ruth and I were making the most of the opportunity to catch up on the emails on our laptops, so we left her to it. After slowly making her way around the room, she stood in front of the mirror for a long time and then went across to our feedback area. On a big sheet of wallpaper, we'd written two simple questions, 'How did you feel?' and 'What did you think?' This is what she wrote:

- *'I have to be honest and say that I never knew what I believed in God, if I did or not, but I feel an "enlightenment", an acceptance in myself. It's nice to feel that there will always be someone to turn to, to offer unconditional love.'*

No one had prayed with her. Embarrassingly, neither Ruth nor I had even spoken with her while she explored the prayer space, and yet something had happened. She'd experienced something of the unconditional love and acceptance of God, and it had changed her.

Despite having heard the amazing stories of the first four prayer spaces, this was way beyond what Ruth, James and I had expected. This simple place of reflection and prayer had become a place of mission, a place where pupils who didn't believe in God were encountering the presence of God and then trying to find language for what they'd experienced. Those who suffered with low self-esteem experienced encouragement: 'It made me feel good about myself.' Those who were grieving experienced comfort: 'I'm sad about my friend dying. It was good to talk and pray about it because I can't talk about it at home.' Those who were struggling with strong emotions experienced peace: 'It helps you calm down when you're angry.' Those who were spiritually searching experienced an unexpected welcome: 'This is a great way to help people pray even if they do not believe in God.' And some just felt good after their visit to the prayer space, which was in itself a gift: 'This is honestly the best thing that has happened to me all day.'

And it wasn't just the pupils who came to find the prayer space. On the Friday afternoon, while all the pupils were in lessons, the reception manager locked the school's front office and brought her whole team to the prayer space. 'The pupils have been talking about this all week as they've passed by,' she said, 'so we've decided to come and see it for ourselves.' Earlier in the week, a teacher had hovered in the doorway for a moment before asking, 'Are there any pupils in here?' When Ruth shook her head, the teacher had quickly come inside and pulled a chair over to where Ruth and James were sitting. She'd started telling them about her failing marriage, and as her tears fell she whispered, 'Please pray for me.' Ruth and James bowed their heads and began to pray for her. In our debrief the following week, James reflected, 'I don't think we were expecting the depth. We weren't expecting the vulnerability, the pain, the sticky note prayers about parents who'd separated, young people who were bereaved, etcetera. Maybe these young people have never had an opportunity like this?'

The Turning Point

As I've said, at this time I was serving as 24–7 Prayer's UK director, which may sound very grand and important, but it mostly meant trying to make sense of the 24–7 Prayer 'stuff' that was going on around the country and then trying to join the dots, wherever possible.

Leadership, I've always felt, begins with a lot of listening and learning, and in 2008, there was a lot to listen to and a lot to learn from.

So one of the things we started hosting was a 24–7 Prayer UK Network Day every six months or so, where people who were leading and shaping the movement in the UK could come together and worship God, swap stories, eat together and pray for one another. We invited people who were leading 24–7 Prayer Rooms for their town or city, or for their church network, and people who were taking the model and using it missionally, setting up prayer rooms on university campuses and in youth centres, in town-centre shopfronts and in touring caravans. We invited people who had launched justice projects, having heard God speak to them in 24–7 Prayer Rooms. And we invited people who were leading what we were calling Boiler Rooms: communities that were developing rhythms of prayer, hospitality and mission together. Over time, some of these Boiler Rooms ended up becoming churches or monastic communities.[3]

In December 2008, our Network Day was in Stanford-le-Hope in Essex. About fifty people had travelled from all over the UK to be with us that day, and Tom Jamieson was one of them, all the way from Ryton in the north-east of England. I asked him to tell some stories from their first 24–7 Prayer Room, and especially about the impact that it had on pupils from the local high school.

Then I talked about the other prayer spaces in schools, including the one Ruth, James and I had just hosted. 'This isn't about getting young people from the schools to join our churches,' I said at the end. 'This is about God calling our churches to serve and seek first the kingdom of heaven in our schools.' I flicked to Matthew 9 in *The Message* and paraphrased aloud: 'When [Jesus] looked out over the school communities – the millions of children and young people – his heart broke. So confused and aimless they were, like sheep with no shepherd. "What a huge harvest!" he said to his disciples. "How few workers! On your knees and pray for harvest hands!"'[4]

And so, we began to pray ... and something happened. Thirty minutes later, all around the old Methodist church hall, people were praying in the corners, down the aisles, between the pews, even on the low stage. Some were kneeling, silently interceding, and many were flat on their faces, weeping and crying out to God on behalf of the younger generation. The presence of God was tangible in the room. I was lying on the floor too, and to be honest, I felt a bit afraid. I looked across at my friend Andy, who was lying near me. 'What's happening?' I whispered. 'What do we do now?' Andy just smiled and shrugged. God was planting something in our hearts – something that would grow and affect tens of thousands of children's and young people's lives in the years to come. The 24–7 Prayer movement had begun with a bold vision to 'turn the tide in youth culture', but maybe God needed to turn a tide in us first . . . to turn our hearts towards children and young people, to allow our hearts to be broken just like Jesus' was.

The Movement Spreads

'So, what are we going to do now?' I asked. It was February 2010, and Tim, Rach and I were sitting around a tiny, slightly sticky table in Harpers Sandwich Bar on Southwark Street in London, just across the road from Borough Market. I think it's now part of the Costa Coffee chain, but back then, Harpers Sandwich Bar was a uniquely British greasy spoon café (pronounced 'kaff') that served doorstep-sized cheese-and-pickle sandwiches and tea and coffee in large mugs for less than a pound. We'd arranged to meet and talk about the prayer spaces that were spreading around the country. After the first four, twelve more prayer spaces had been created in schools the following year, and another forty the year after that.

'We need to help those who want to get started. Have either of you got a pen?' I asked as I grabbed a paper napkin from the dispenser. On it, we scribbled the names of friends who had already hosted prayer spaces in their schools, and the Christian organisations that had been in touch to talk about partnering in some way. And then we began to sketch some early ideas for a website, as well as for some kind of national networking day to swap stories and deliver basic training. That napkin was our first strategic plan. (I still have it, tucked away in one of my journals.)

It took a lot longer to build and launch the first Prayer Spaces in Schools website than we'd anticipated, and so we created an interim resource pack PDF. In it, we gathered the experiences of those who'd already run prayer spaces in their schools, we drafted guidelines for getting started, we listed some example prayer activities, and we included a few case studies, and then we sent it out to the hundred or so people who'd contacted us asking for help. This PDF became known, rather unimaginatively, as the '9 Step Guide to Running Great Prayer Spaces', and one of the people we sent it to was Catherine Clayton, a primary school RE coordinator in Oxfordshire.

Catherine's Story

When Catherine discovered that one of her colleagues was also a Christian, they decided to start praying together. Catherine asked the head teacher if they could use a classroom for their little prayer group, and to her surprise, the head not only said yes, but added that she'd like to join in. Sometime later, the head told Catherine that she'd rediscovered her faith during their prayer group meetings.

Other Christians started to join in, and Catherine wondered what to do with her growing prayer group. Then she received an email from the children's worker at her church in Oxford, saying; 'I've heard about this thing called prayer spaces in schools, and you're a teacher, so I thought you should do it.' Catherine emailed the 24–7 Prayer office and we sent her our 40-page '9 Step Guide' PDF, and her first thought was, 'No, that's not happening. I don't have time to read this!', so she deleted it.

A month later though, Catherine found herself thinking about the possibility of hosting a prayer space in her school and so she emailed us to ask for the PDF once again. When she presented the idea to the school prayer group, the head teacher was the first to say, 'Let's do this!' And so they did. Catherine and her team hosted their first prayer space in March 2010. It was open from Monday to Friday, and it really was amazing. When I asked Catherine what she remembers most from that first prayer space, she replied immediately, 'Opening it to parents after school . . . watching them doing the prayer activities with their children.

'I enjoyed organising the prayer space. I liked the excitement and the creativity. I liked having people from different churches, helping them to serve and work together. I obviously didn't have time to be in the prayer space all the time, so I rang all the local churches and recruited volunteers to come and help "host" the prayer space. The teachers did the input bit, and the church volunteers hosted the prayer activities – it really worked.

'I remember popping into the prayer space at the end of one of the school days to find the Special Education Needs (SEN) teacher kneeling beside the Bubble Tube. "It's great to be here and be still for a while before I have to go home," she said. One of the Anglican vicars told me that he "loved the space". There were lots of important moments, and not just for the children. The children loved our prayer space, of course, but it was the impact beyond the children that really excited me – the prayer group rising to the occasion and leading the way, engaging local church communities in service and mission.'

Two months later, Catherine handed in her notice and quit her job as a teacher so that she could encourage and equip churches across Oxfordshire to set up prayer spaces in partnership with their local schools.

'Don't worry if you only manage to get two or three new prayer spaces started this year,' I said, trying to be encouraging. But by the end of the year, she'd kick-started ten, and that was just the beginning. Things multiplied, as they tended to around Catherine. Before long, she'd launched a local charity called BeSpace, which has since supported 700 prayer spaces in over 160 schools – that's more than a third of all the schools in Oxfordshire.

'And what story sticks in your mind? What would be your memorable moment from a prayer space?' I once asked her over coffee.

'Oh, that's easy,' she replied. 'It was a sticky note I read, where a child had written, "This made me feel free." I thought, wow, how can five minutes in a prayer space do this? What must life be like for a child to say something like that? But then again, *every* prayer space I've visited has felt like this, and nothing else that I've experienced comes close to that feeling. People engaging with God and themselves. It's exciting and creative. It's liberating.'

Reflect and Pray

1. At the start of this chapter, I talked about feeling deeply unsettled in my work role. Although I didn't recognise the signs at the time, God was calling me into something new. Are there any areas where you are feeling unsettled at the moment? Ask God to speak to you, and listen carefully.

2. The pupil who wrote that the prayer space had 'opened up religion into my life again' may have previously been involved with a church. Think of a young person you know who has left a church and/or their faith behind. Ask God to speak to them.

3. Catherine's incredible story began with a small group of Christians praying for the school where they all worked. If you're not already part of a small group like this, why not start one?

PRAYER ACTIVITY: LETTERS FROM GOD

Ruth, James and I used the Letter from God prayer activity in our first prayer space and we were amazed at some of the letters that pupils wrote. Here are the details.

What is it?

People of most faiths believe that God sometimes speaks through the words and actions of particular people. These people God speaks through are usually called prophets. This activity encourages pupils to imagine what God might want to say to their school or their local community, their town/city, their nation, or the world. You will be amazed at some of the things the pupils write!

How does it work?

This activity works best if you choose up to three situations or locations – for example, your school community, your town/city, your nation. Gather a bit of background material to help pupils connect with these three situations or locations, such as photographs, data/statistics, news stories and so on. Pre-print some A5 sheets titled 'Letter from God' and provide some pens or pencils.

Stick the photos and the other information about the school, town/city or nation on the walls and the table, alongside the A5 'Letter from God . . .' sheets and the pens/pencils.

Who is it for?

This activity works well with primary-aged children (aged seven to eleven) and secondary-aged young people (aged twelve to sixteen).

Any other information?

This prayer activity can be presented in a variety of ways, depending on the setting and the season – for example, a letter from God, a Christmas card from God, a love letter from God.

Some pupils find it hard to switch from expressing their own prayers to considering what God (whether they believe in God or not) might want to say. This activity works best, therefore, with a team member alongside them to clarify the purpose and the instructions. (You will need to check the letters from time to time for anything inappropriate.)

Instructions

Look at the information about your school, your town and your nation. Whether you believe in God or not, imagine that God wrote a letter to your school, your town or your country, or even to you. What do you think God would say in it? Think carefully . . .

If you want to, you can write on one of the printed 'Letter from God' sheets – you can write the letter to your school, or your town, or your country, or to yourself; it's up to you. When you've finished, add your letter to the display.

A little story . . .

Instead of telling you a story, here are a few of the Letters from God that pupils wrote in the prayer space that Ruth, James and I hosted:

'If you have a problem you can tell me
I will listen and not judge.
God xxx'

'When times get rough
there is ALWAYS someone to turn to.
Your friends, family, teachers,
other pupils, and ME!
Don't be afraid and always believe in my
UNCONDITIONAL LOVE'

'Be yourself and don't be afraid of what you are.
Be yourself!!'

'No matter what
I will love you
but will you trust me?
God xx'

'Dear child,
I don't want your CV.
You are enough.
Love, God'

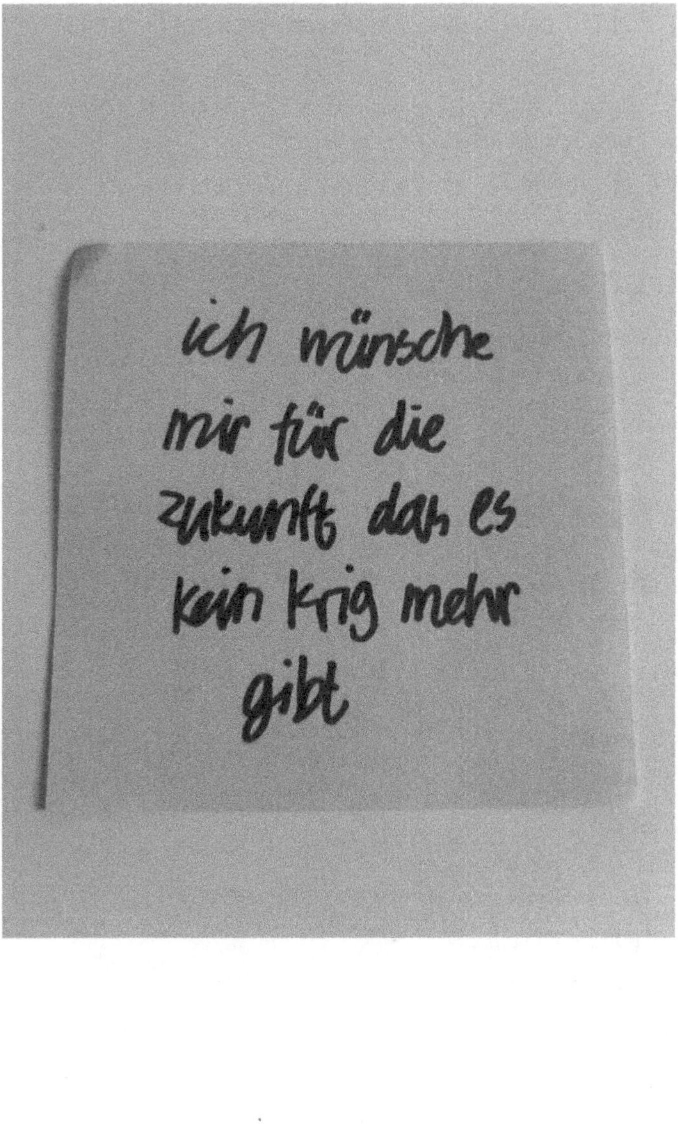
ich wünsche
mir für die
zukunft daß es
kein krig mehr
gibt

3

Isi . . . and the Rest of the World

What pupils say: *'It was soooo cool. I now no longer believe that anything is impossible for God.'*—Isi, aged fourteen, Germany

What church leaders say: *'We have a whole generation of young Catholics who are religiously aware but spiritually dead. We need something that will bring them to life. I think prayer spaces might be part of the answer.'*—Father Paul Chetcuti, Catholic Archdiocese of Malta

Introducing Isi

'What did you think of the conference?' I asked.

'It was amazing,' replied fourteen-year-old Isi, and then her smile faded a bit, 'but we could never do something like this in my school in Germany.'

Neither of us could have possibly imagined that just four months later Isi would be standing in front of some of her friends, explaining how to use the prayer space that she'd set up in one of the school classrooms. And not only that, but that her prayer space in the small town of Ehringshausen would become the first fruit of a growing movement in schools across Germany, and in many other nations too.

Nothing is Impossible

For the second Prayer Spaces in Schools Conference in 2012 we went back to St James Church in Clerkenwell, in central London. There were about 150 people in the hall, but the big surprise was discovering that three of them had flown from Germany (very!) early that morning. One was a teacher, one was a youth worker, and between them sat fourteen-year-old Isi.

The youth worker's name was Jana Nimmo, and she was from Marburg, which is roughly in the centre of Germany, a little to the west. Jana stayed overnight with my family after the conference, and we went out for coffee the following morning. 'I got to know Isi just a few days before we came,' Jana explained. 'Someone sponsored three of us to come to England and I wanted to bring a teacher and a pupil. I was visiting a little prayer group at a school about thirty miles from Marburg and I asked if any of them wanted to come. Isi said, "Why not?" and when she asked her parents, they said yes, so we came!' Another coincidence? It felt like God was up to something and so, as we sat in the coffee shop together, we prayed . . . for Isi, for Jana, and for prayer spaces to start in Germany.

After returning from her trip to London, Isi just couldn't get the prayer space idea out of her head, so she approached the head teacher at her school and asked if she could set one up. To her surprise, he said yes, and so she immediately started making plans and gathering materials. A few weeks later, when the prayer space was over, Isi wrote me a long, excited email, which tells the story a lot better than I ever could, so . . . over to Isi:

> In the morning of the prayerspaceday, I was sooo excited and nervous . . . it was terrible. I think the most frightening bit for me was presenting the room to the classes, especially the classes from my year group.
>
> Do you remember when we were in England and I was so sceptical? I thought, how will it work to have a prayer space in our school? Will pupils come there and pray?! Will they be quiet? Well . . . God is very weird. He did all better than I thought. :D The classes came in and they were quiet. They went to the prayer activities and they wrote things down. They showed respect (after some scepticism in the beginning).
>
> I was soooo excited!! And then, the people came in, gave me attention and it went well! It was so fascinating

to see 25 pupils who are a little bit confused when they first come into the room, who maybe laugh about something, and then they really start to think about their lives! BAAAAM!!

We had six prayer activities:

+ The Biggest Dream
+ A clothes line where you could hang notes about what you are thankful for
+ Pray The News (a poster with news from all over the world)
+ Be Sorry (using Magna Doodles)
+ Be Yourself (using mirrors on a wall)
+ Something where you could put on your questions to God

I did the first two classes, and then Philipp, the guy who was helping me, did the next two classes. He's about 12, and he was also veeeery nervous, but he did it soooooo well! All the people who took part in the prayerspace could experience God there, and we all went beyond our borders because God makes the impossible possible. Wow, that sounds poetic, but I'm serious!

A few days later Anna (she's 14) said to me, 'Ooh Isi, since Wednesday I have such joy and fire in my heart!' That's sooo amazing!! Haha, something else made me laugh. A girl who comes to our Bible club, but isn't a Christian, said, 'Ooh, it's very cosy and beautiful here, I thought it would be boring.'

The things that really touched me were the questions that they asked God, like:

+ 'Why is there so much sorrow in the world?' – asked very often
+ 'Why does my mum have to feel so much pain?'
+ 'Why does nobody accept me the way I am?'
+ 'If not you are responsible for the sorrow in the world, who is?'
+ 'If you exist, show me!'

The teachers had positive opinions about it too. One of them is a little bit weird and I don't really know what he believes, but it was funny because he started a conversation with our youth group leader who came along for the day. The teacher came back with classes three times, just so he could go on with their conversation.

Towards the end of her email, Isi told me an extraordinary story. After visiting the prayer space, one of the teachers took his class into another room to talk about what they thought and how they felt about their experience. He asked if any of them prayed regularly, and after a long silence, one boy put up his hand and said, 'I pray the Lord's Prayer every night.' The whole class erupted into laughter, and amid the noise someone shouted, 'If that's true, then say it by heart!' The boy slowly stood to his feet and began to pray, '*Vater unser im Himmel, geheiligt werde dein Name . . .*' The laughter faded almost immediately, and the whole class fell silent as he recited line after line of the prayer that Jesus taught his disciples. And then, as he finished, his classmates burst into applause!

'I never thought it could happen this way,' Isi wrote at the end of her email. 'It's weird and sooo cool, since we've done this I think nothing is impossible, and I can do anything with God. :D :D'

Germany

Isi's was the first prayer space in Germany, but it certainly wasn't the last. The Christian organisation that Jana worked for at the time, Schüler-SMD, asked her to deliver some prayer space training for their school workers around the country, and I flew over to help. Schüler-SMD mostly worked with schools and pupils directly, rather than with local churches, so we had to do some creative thinking around the model, but it wasn't long before other pilot prayer spaces were popping up around Germany.

'It was the stories from the pupils that really moved

me,' Jana told me in an email, before listing some examples from the first few prayer spaces (translated into English, thankfully; my German language skills aren't great, yet):

'It was a very special atmosphere in here.'

'What I liked most was the activity where I could write down my sorrows. At home I never pray. There are things in my life that I can't tell anybody.'

'I felt so free. Like never before.'

'I'm more relaxed now and happy because I was able to switch off after all the stress of school.'

'I noticed that there are a lot of people who have more problems than me and others who have fewer problems than me. Some also have the same problems. I don't feel so excluded and alone.'

As I read these quotes, it struck me that pupils in Germany were saying and praying the same things as those in England (albeit in a different language). They were expressing the same hopes and aspirations, the same anxieties about themselves, the same struggles in their relationships, the same grief, the same loneliness, the same anger about issues of injustice. And they were expressing the same questions about the world, and about God. I found myself wondering if we would find the same thing in other nations too.

Fast-forward a few years, and Jana is now the national coordinator for Prayerspaces in Schulen which is part of 24–7 Prayer in Germany, but also a standalone charity with its own board, leadership team, website and training opportunities. She estimates that they have supported more than 250 prayer spaces in schools since Isi's, and the opportunities are continuing to grow.

When I asked Jana for her favourite moment – a prayer space story that will stay with her forever – she told me about a twelve-year-old boy who 'was asked to imagine what God might write in a letter to him. This was his response: 'Dear Peter. When are you finally coming to me? I am waiting for you. God.'

Malta

I've got quite a lot of Catholic friends, but Father Paul Chetcuti and Father Reuben Gauci were the first Catholic priests to come and stay in our home, which they did in 2009. As we ate together, we exchanged introductions, compared cultural uniquenesses and eventually got to talking about prayer spaces. Paul explained that his role included coordinating the

Spiritual Development in Schools (SDS) team in Malta and that he was interested in introducing prayer spaces to them. 'I have recently held a meeting with teachers involved in the spiritual animation[1] and chaplaincy work in church schools,' he explained. 'They were enthusiastic even when I just hinted at this experiment.'

I was deeply impressed as I listened to Paul and Reuben talk about the work their teams were doing in nearly all of the Catholic and state schools in their island-nation of 600,000 people. There was a passion in the way they communicated, and they had plenty of creative projects on the go. So why had they travelled all this way to the UK? It didn't make much sense to me, so I asked them, 'Why are you here? What are you looking for?' Paul thought for a moment, as if savouring the question.

'Phil,' he said, suddenly serious. 'In Malta, we have a whole generation of young Catholics who are religiously aware, but they are spiritually dead. We need something that will bring them to life. I think prayer spaces might be part of the answer.'

* * *

A few months later, Paul and Reuben invited me to go to Malta (I know, I know, poor me – but sometimes following Jesus involves shouldering our personal crosses and walking the path of suffering!) to deliver some prayer space training to a group of educators, priests and catechists. They expected about forty people to sign up and show up, but in the end we had 225 participants across three whole days, and a national TV network even came along to film some of it too.

One of the educators in the room was Silvana Cardona. She was working in a state learning support centre for fourteen- to sixteen-year-old boys with social, emotional and behavioural difficulties, and as she listened to the stories of prayer spaces in the UK, she realised that there were some similarities with the centre's therapeutic educational approach. She felt inspired to try hosting a prayer space at her centre and, because she is a go-do-it kind of person, she immediately went and did it.

Silvana's centre could only accommodate a maximum of fifteen boys at that time and, given the level of support that the boys needed, the educator-to-pupil ratio was very high too. With this in mind, Silvana set up the prayer space in a small hall and planned to take the boys to it in groups of three or four. 'But they were still embarrassed and shy,' she explained when we spoke on the phone. 'They picked on each other and made fun of each other, and they wouldn't do any of the activities. At first I was disappointed, but then, later on that first day, one boy asked me and another colleague if we would reopen the prayer space for him so he could experience it on his own. The boy spent about thirty minutes in the prayer space, using the creative activities and experiencing the stillness. Afterwards, he said that he didn't even notice the time had passed, and he told us that it felt really good. Other boys started asking to do the same thing, and many of them also came back during break times as well to continue using the prayer activities.

'One boy told me that he didn't want to write his Big Question prayer onto a piece of torn-up card-board because his question was "too heavy", and he asked me if he could write it onto a stone instead. When I said yes, he took a marker pen and wrote his prayer onto the stone, and then he hid it in front of an image of Jesus on the cross. He told me that his family were all in prison and that he'd written a prayer about them.'

Day after day, the boys returned to the prayer space. Silvana was amazed by how seriously they were taking it, and how deeply they were engaging with the activities, even though it was uncomfortable at times. 'One boy wrote, "Why did you create me?" And then he swore at God. We realised that these were honest prayers though, and that it must be OK to talk honestly with God.' (It's uncomfortable to hear or read prayers like these, but we'll return to the question of expressing anger and pain in prayer in Chapter 8.)

Prayer spaces quickly became a regular feature at the learning support centre. On one occasion, Silvana invited a local primary school to send some classes along for a visit. 'I asked some of our boys if they would help me to welcome the children and show them around. One in particular helped a lot – he seemed to really enjoy it. He was doing the leadership unit of his Prince's Trust International Achievement course at the time, so this became his practical application. As far as I know, he now works in childcare.'

In an email that Silvana sent to me a few weeks ago, she wrote:

> Every prayer space has affected me. Yesterday, I was preparing some prayer activities and as I wrote out the instruction cards, I began to weep. I feel the pain of the children and young people who use these prayer activities, and I experience God's healing through them too. It is always part of the process. Whenever I am in a prayer space, I don't just read the sticky notes and the torn-up cardboard, but I pray for the children and young people. I join my prayers with theirs. Children need space like this to find God, to communicate with God. It's within their reach – they just need the opportunity and the encouragement. There's a spiritual spark within

> every child and young person. And it's not just in the pupils, but in the teachers and the parents too. Teachers often ask if they can return to the prayer space. If they hadn't experienced something deep and real, they wouldn't ask to come back!

Since Silvana created the prayer space at the learning support centre, there have been hundreds more prayer spaces in schools on their tiny island, and every year, Reuben and the SDS team train dozens more educators, priests and catechists to host new ones. We used to joke that Malta would probably be first to reach the lofty/seemingly impossible goal of having a prayer space in every school. But then, not long ago, Reuben told me that according to their latest data there have been prayer spaces in 67 per cent of all schools (60 per cent of state schools and 75 per cent of Catholic schools) . . . so we don't joke about it any more!

Silvana is now a pastoral worker with the SDS team in Malta and she's written a short illustrated story book[2] for younger children based on some of the prayer activities. Together, the team have integrated prayer activities into a range of literacy programmes and educational materials around understanding and expressing emotions. They've also adapted prayer space ideas in all sorts of new ways,[3] and they've even developed outdoor summer schools by designing prayer activities that are themed around specific locations. Mind you, it must help when you can say something like, 'And now, at the spot where the apostle Paul was shipwrecked on his way to Italy,[4] let's reflect on how it feels when things don't work out quite the way we've planned . . .'!

* * *

From the tiny island of Malta, Reuben and the SDS team have been delivering training to, and sharing prayer-space stories with, Catholic colleagues in many nations around the world. They, like we in other nations, can sometimes trace where enquiries have come from, but a lot of the time we can't. People seem to be finding their own way to our websites and social media channels, getting inspired by the stories and then starting their own prayer spaces.

In the week that I'm writing this chapter, I've had video calls and exchanged emails and messages with people who are already hosting prayer spaces in schools, or who are figuring out how to get started, from the following nations: France, India, Austria, Australia, Ireland, the Czech Republic, Peru, South Africa, South Korea and the USA. In addition to these, we've tracked and supported prayer spaces in schools in Romania, Hong Kong, the Cayman Islands, Canada, Uganda, New Zealand, the Netherlands and Hungary, to name just a few. Sadly, I don't have the space to tell you about all of them, but as we close this chapter, let's take a few snapshots . . .

India

In the north of India, Davie and a team of volunteers set up a prayer space for an international school. The room they were using was an awkward hexagonal shape, but they decided to make the most of it by using each of the internal walls for different activities. By the end of the week you could barely see any of the wall surfaces because they were all covered in sticky note prayers. When Davie asked a few of the pupils how they felt and what they thought about their first prayer space, they said things like:

'I feel like I can be myself here, I feel like I'm loved.'

'My favourite activity was the one with the mirrors – it's the first time I've felt valued.'

'I like that we can write our prayers and no-one is there to judge us.'

'When I go into the prayer space it feels like I don't have to worry about anything.'

Austria

Catholic priest Mag. Michael Scharf was working for the Archdiocese of Vienna when he invited us to deliver some prayer space training for his interns. Shortly afterwards, Michael hosted the first prayer space in a school in Austria, which he called Soulspace. The feedback was amazing, and the idea quickly spread to other schools. One of his interns, Franz Greisberger, relocated to Salzburg, where he worked for the Catholic Youth team. Franz soon had them running prayer spaces in schools too, and they called theirs ALIVE! Franz now works as the head teacher in a Protestant school in Salzburg, and he is also our national coordinator, offering support and training to the Catholic diocese and to individuals all over Austria.

> 'It rarely happens in student work that independently, from so many different sides, you hear of something new that's making waves. Whether it's colleagues from Schüler-SMD in Germany, or the children's pastoral team from the Catholic Diocese of Vienna, or a Protestant religious teacher from the Austrian town of Steyr, or for the European IFS Schülbeweger Network Meeting in Hungary, everywhere you go, people are talking about prayer spaces in schools.'—*Scripture Union Austria* (national newsletter)

South Africa

When Jason Stanier and the Youth In Transformation (YIT) team that he leads in Cape Town hosted their first prayer space in a school, they were overwhelmed by the response of the pupils. Jason asked his team for any memorable moments, and one young woman described a board that they'd set up with pictures of gang violence. 'The kids looked at the pictures and then said a prayer for family members who had been affected by gang violence, or for the safety of our community, or for gang leaders to turn away from what they were doing, and then the pupils could tie a ribbon around a frame that we'd built. I had a moment with a young girl. I asked her if she knew what gangsters were, and she said that her dad had been killed by one last year. It broke my heart. It's amazing to have a space where they can talk about their trauma and also pray through that process. I think there were at least three girls who had lost their fathers, and I watched one of them drawing a picture of herself with her dad at the People Tree prayer activity. We just don't understand what these kids have been through.'

Jason himself was deeply moved by what they had experienced. 'I've been a youth worker for a long time,' he said, 'but I've never experienced anything quite like this. It's like doing a whole year of youth ministry in just one week.' Jason is now our national coordinator in South Africa, and prayer spaces are beginning to spread.

The USA

Darnell has been a pastor in Milwaukee, the most populous city in the US state of Wisconsin, for more than twenty years, and his family have been involved with 24–7 Prayer in the USA for some of that time. When he was in their prayer room one day, praying for ten of the local high schools, Darnell felt he should reach out to them. So he sent them all a letter, offering to help, and almost immediately he received a reply from the community coordinator in one of the schools – probably the most challenging school in the area – asking to set up a video call.

'I didn't even know what a community coordinator was at the time,' Darnell admitted, when I interviewed him during one of our online training seminars, 'but I soon learned that her role is to represent what the students want and need, and to work with community groups and parents who can help and give input. So, I sent her a link to one of the Prayer Spaces in Schools websites and a video of our prayer room, and to be honest I didn't expect to hear anything more from her, but to my surprise and delight, she said yes, and the principal said yes too. "We want you to come and host a Quiet Space in our school!" they said.

'When I went into the school the next week, I was expecting them to offer me a dusty closet for the Quiet Space. But then they showed me the room they'd chosen and it was huge. It was also just down from the cafeteria, so there was a lot of traffic, and it was right next to the sex education room too. God has a sense of humour and God is strategic! There were a lot of things we had to go through – background checks and stuff – and we worked hard to build good relationships with the staff and the security guards and everyone in the school. I've been a pastor for a long time – it's all, and it's always, about relationships. Anyway, we eventually got the Quiet Space set up with the prayer activities, the fairy lights and everything, and we were ready to get started.

'Just before we opened it, the community coordinator arranged for me to meet with the seven or eight young people who were on the student council. We started talking and then one of them said to me, "We've been asking the principal for a space where we can get out of classes – a lot of students suffer with anxiety and sometimes we just need to step away for a bit." I couldn't believe it. "Come with me!" I said, and we went down to the Quiet Space together. When I opened the door it was like we all suddenly felt the presence of God. The kids started crying! Even the community coordinator was wiping her eyes. They were emotional and excited too. One of the girls said a strange thing – I'll never forget it. She said, "This is like a secret place." Another one said, "This shouldn't just be for bad kids, for those on suspension – this should be for all of us."

'The following week, we opened the Quiet Space for the very first time and it's been open pretty much ever since – our team goes in to host it every Wednesday and Thursday, from 9 a.m. until 2:30 p.m. At first, the community coordinator just wanted the school psychologists and social workers to make referrals, to choose the kids who would come and visit the room. However, more recently, class tutors have been referring the kids too – I think the school has realised what that young girl knew from the start, that the Quiet Space should be for everyone.'

Start Where You Are

To the south-west of Milwaukee, in Kansas City, Missouri, Katie was invited to make a place of 'safety, rest, and peace' for the teachers at her daughter's school. It's a private Christian school in a particularly disadvantaged area, and in Katie's words, 'the kids in this neighbourhood often lack the resources and opportunities given to kids in other districts. More often than not they have been deeply affected by racial, socioeconomic and educational disparities. The school is trying to bridge those gaps, but it's hard work.'

Katie immediately accepted the invitation. She'd come to love the whole school community, and she felt like God was calling her to serve in some way, so she was delighted to be able to set up the prayer space for staff, who she felt really needed some encouragement. 'It was amazing!' she wrote afterwards. 'The teachers come from various backgrounds and they had never experienced anything like it. Some of them were quiet and they methodically engaged with each activity, one by one. Others came in and stayed at just one activity for the entire time, weeping. I had a team – myself and two of the leaders from church – and we were available to help welcome people to the room, and pray with them if they wanted us to.

'One exciting thing is that we had two public school teachers visit who'd heard about the prayer space and wanted to experience it. One was so impacted by it that we began talking about what it would look like to have a space available in his school for students and staff. He was blown away by the personal impact and excited about how something similar could work in public schools.'

Over the coming months, I suspect that people in other parts of the USA will adopt or adapt Darnell's Quiet Space model, because it seems to be one that works. It will also be interesting to see if another model emerges from Katie's conversations with her new friends from the public schools in Kansas City. Elsewhere, we've heard from workers in Christian schools in Texas who are using prayer activities during lunchtime clubs in some of the schools where they have good relationships. And we're also figuring out how to support Christian pupils who want to set up prayer spaces in their schools. Isi has already demonstrated that this is possible in Germany, so why not in the USA? Friends in lots of places there – from Tulsa to Detroit, and from Portland, Oregon, to New York City – are dreaming and scheming (and praying) for ways to host prayer spaces, so . . . watch this space!

* * *

If you're not from the UK, and especially if you're from a nation where prayer spaces aren't yet taking place in schools, I hope that you feel . . . well, hope. I hope you feel encouraged by the stories you've read about people in different nations, with very different education systems and different cultural contexts (both in the church and in wider society), who are all finding ways to adapt the prayer space principles and practices and make them work where they are. While lots of things are different in each nation, the need and the hunger among children and young people for prayer spaces seems to be the same wherever you go. As Silvana said, 'Children need space like this to find God, to communicate with God.'

So here are a few practical suggestions to help you get started:

- *Pray.* Start by talking with God about the schools where you are. Ask God to give you wisdom and discernment around the best ways that you can serve those school communities. And remember, nothing is impossible. Or, to put it another way . . . things that seem to be impossible now might not be impossible forever.
- *Get in touch.* We already have national coordinators in a few nations, and we have good friends in many more. There may be people who are already praying and talking about getting started with prayer spaces in schools in your nation whom we can connect you with. Visit the Prayer Spaces in Schools website[5] and send us a message.
- *Do some research.* Learn about the education system in your nation, or in your region/state. What are its priorities? What are its felt needs? Where are the doorways, the opportunities for Christians to serve school communities (from outside, or from within)? Ask Christian teachers and other education professionals what they think.

- *Get creative.* Adopt ideas that others are using. Adapt them to fit your context. Take the prayer space principles and practices and make them work where you are.
- *Do it!* Go on . . . you can do it. (Let us know how it goes!)

Reflect and Pray

1. Isi said, 'Since we've done this I think nothing is impossible, and I can do anything with God.' What feels impossible right now, especially in relation to getting started with prayer spaces? Talk with God about this.

2. The simple, creative prayer spaces that Silvana set up at her learning centre had a big impact on young boys with very complex needs. Prayer really does change lives. If you know a child or a young person who is really struggling with social, emotional or behavioural issues, why don't you pray for them now? Maybe you could find a small stone and write their name on it (a bit like the boy you read about earlier), and then hide it somewhere at home as a reminder to continue praying for them.

3. As you've read this chapter, which of the nations I've mentioned has particularly caught your attention? Or is there another nation that is in your mind or on your heart? A good friend of mine says that we should pray our best prayers for others instead of ourselves. Pause now and pray your biggest, best prayer for the nation that you're thinking of – for God to do incredible things in the lives of children and young people in schools there.

PRAYER ACTIVITY: BE SORRY

In Isi's prayer space, one of the activities was called Be Sorry. Pupils wrote the things that they were sorry about on a magnetic board, and then they wiped it clean again afterwards. There are lots of different ways to help children and young people to express saying sorry. Here are a couple of examples:

What is it?

Saying sorry is an act of humility. It is about acknowledging that we have said or done something wrong, and it is part of the process of putting things right. This activity invites pupils to write something that they've said or done wrong recently on a whiteboard, or in a tray of sand, and then wipe it away again. Saying sorry helps to restore broken relationships.

How does it work?

For this activity, you will need:

- EITHER a whiteboard, some whiteboard pens and a dry cloth
- OR a tray of damp sand. (It's a good idea to put a plastic sheet beneath the tray, so that the sand doesn't go everywhere.)

Who is it for?

This activity works with any age group. We're never too young or too old to say sorry.

Instructions

When we do or say something that we know is wrong, it's important to say sorry. Saying sorry is about starting to put things right.

If you want to, you can write or draw what you are sorry about on the whiteboard (or in the tray of sand). Or you can just write the word 'sorry' as you think about what you've said or done. When you feel ready, wipe it clean again. Christians believe that when we say sorry, God forgives us. If what you said or did hurt someone else, you may want to say sorry to the person as well.

A little story . . .

A class of fourteen- to fifteen-year-olds were coming to the end of their visit to the prayer space that had been set up in a Church of England school's drama studio. One of the girls asked if she could speak with the teacher, and then led her across to a large wooden cross that they were using as a Be Sorry activity.

'I want to show you my sorry prayer,' she said. 'I know I don't have to, but I feel like I should tell someone.' She pointed to a small yellow note pinned to the cross, on which the teacher read these words: 'I'm sorry for egging your house.' Seeing the puzzled look on the teacher's face, the girl explained, somewhat guiltily, 'I threw eggs at a church!' The teacher told me later that it required a lot of effort to stifle a giggle at this confession.

Part 2

An Explanation . . . the Ministry of Reconciliation

As prayer spaces continued to spread into schools around the UK, and into many other nations too, I found myself asking lots of questions: What was happening? How were children and young people using prayer spaces, especially those who weren't Christians? Was it all prayer? (Did it matter if it wasn't?) What was God doing? And where did we go from here? How could we continue to serve and steward this growing movement?

I needed to find some answers to these (and many other) questions so that I could confidently explain to those who were asking not just *how* to host prayer spaces in schools, but *why* too. And that's what this next part of the book is all about. Just to prepare you, it begins at a slower pace. But I'm sure you'll agree that slowing down is important, because it can be hard to see clearly when things are moving quickly. Just like the children and young people who were participating in prayer spaces in their schools week in, week out, as a team, we too needed to pause, to reflect, to ask some questions and to listen for God's guidance. (Don't worry, there are plenty more stories later on.)

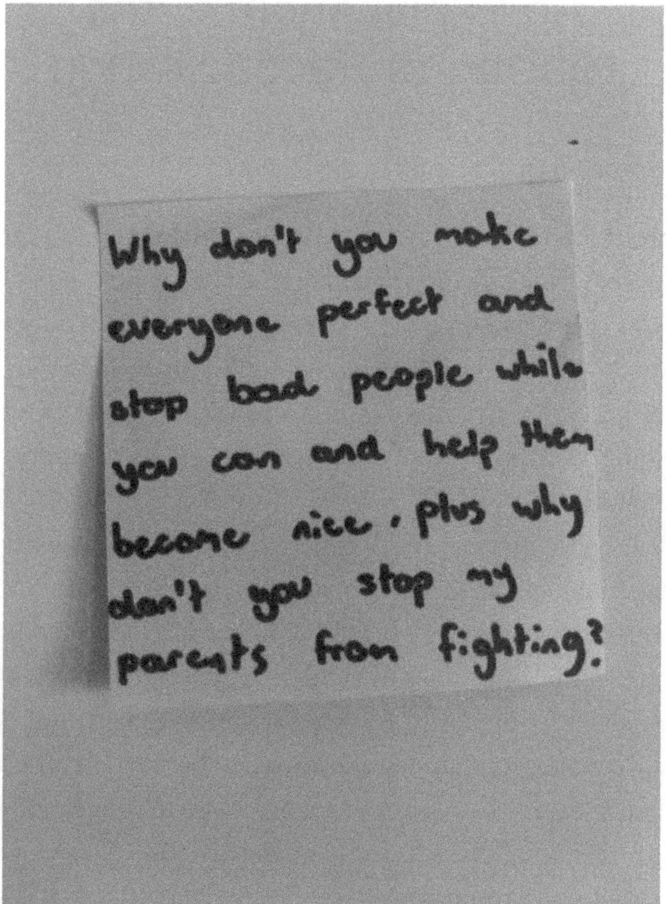
Why don't you make
everyone perfect and
stop bad people while
you can and help them
become nice. plus why
don't you stop my
parents from fighting?

4

Tea with the Professor

What pupils say: *'It's like that feeling . . . like you are stepping on holy ground.'*—Boy, aged eleven

What academics say: *'We can report that the evidence suggests that prayer space activities do indeed contribute to the spiritual development of children and young people who participate. Prayer spaces contribute to all aspects of relational spirituality.'*—Professor Julian Stern, UK[1]

Mission Statements

If you've ever had to write a mission statement for a church or a school or an organisation that you've worked with, I sympathise. Crafting a short sentence or two that describes the purpose of a church/organisation should be fairly easy, but somehow it never is. I spent a few hours in a café in Paddington railway station in London with Catherine, Tim, Rach and a couple of others trying to come up with our first one for Prayer Spaces in Schools. And even then we actually ended up with two mission statements instead of just one – the first for the organisation, and the second for the prayer spaces themselves.

Here's the first statement:

Prayer Spaces in Schools equips local Christians to serve the ongoing spiritual and pastoral life of their school communities by hosting great prayer spaces.

It sounds simple, but every part of this twenty-four-word statement says something important about why Prayer Spaces in Schools exists:

'Prayer Spaces in Schools equips . . .' Prayer Spaces in Schools (the organisation) doesn't set up or host prayer spaces in schools – local Christians do. We just do everything we can to equip them to host really good ones.

'local Christians . . .' These could be volunteers from churches or schools, members of schoolswork organisations, local parents, school staff, pupils, and so on. The key word is *local*, because local relationships are usually closer relationships.

'to serve . . .' We equip local Christians to *serve* school communities, to add value to them, to be a blessing, to be good news.

'the ongoing . . .' Prayer spaces work best when they are offered as part of an ongoing relationship between local Christians and school communities, and not as an annual 'mission week'.

'spiritual and pastoral life . . .' As well as creating safe spaces for spiritual exploration, prayer spaces are also recognised as having a positive impact on pupils' mental and emotional health and on their relationships. Seeking first the kingdom of heaven in people's lives involves all of this (and lots more).

'of their school communities . . .' Over the years, we've discovered that prayer spaces aren't just for pupils. They're also for teachers and other support staff, parents and carers, cleaners and caretakers – the whole school community.

'by hosting great prayer spaces . . .' Hopefully that bit is obvious.

And why schools? Well, for one, if we really want to see our communities transformed by the love of God, the presence of Jesus and the power of the Holy Spirit, then we need to be *in* our communities (and not just in our church buildings). We need to go and serve and be good news and seek first the kingdom of heaven *in* the places through which the local community flows. Schools, surely, should be high on this list.

And here's the second statement:

Prayer spaces enable children and young people, of all faiths and none, to explore spirituality, faith and life's big questions in a safe, creative and interactive way.

Twenty-seven words this time. I still don't know how and why these statements took us so long to formulate, but the book you're holding is my attempt to explain and unpack this statement and to ensure that your prayer spaces fulfil it.

Spiritual

One of the themes that pops up in both statements is the word spiritual (or spirituality), and this is tricky because it's a hard word to define. Theologians, educators and psychologists have a go from time to time, but their definitions often leave you feeling a little bit like saying, 'Yes, but . . .'

When the English scholar of spirituality Jack Priestley was asked whether he could define spirituality, he replied, 'The only honest answer to the question must be a categorical "No". The spiritual is describable but not definable for to define is to set limitations, to draw boundaries.'[2] He then quoted from John 3, 'The wind blows wherever it pleases. You hear its sound, but you cannot tell where it comes from or where it is going. So it is with everyone born of the Spirit.'[3]

One of the few things that many professionals do seem to agree on, however, is that every child is born spiritual. Children's spirituality is 'already there, to be cherished, rather than something to be added on'[4] (a bit like pre-installed, switched-on software on a new laptop), and you can see evidence of it in the holistic way that children see and receive the world, in their openness and curiosity, in their capacity for wonder, in their acceptance of mystery and impossibility, in their quest to learn, in their desire to connect with others, and so on.

Writer and researcher Rebecca Nye describes it like this: 'Children's spirituality is an initial natural capacity for awareness of the sacred quality to life experiences,'[5] and she insists that we need to learn 'to view spirituality as something we expect in every child, rather than something unusual'.[6] Spirituality and spiritual searching are part of every child's God-made identity – they're at the heart of who children are, and they're what hold everything else together.

However, Nye goes on to say that this 'initial natural capacity' for spirituality seems to fade as we get older. It gets 'impeded, crushed, thwarted – stopped from developing'[7] because of suffering and trauma and other adverse life experiences. Furthermore, we can starve our own spirituality by the choices we make, by ignoring the deep yearning for wonder and mystery and relationship inside us, and by filling those spaces and feeding that hunger with less worthy things.

But this doesn't have to be the end of the story – it can be reversed. When people ask about the impact that prayer spaces have on children's and young people's lives, one of the things I often say is that I believe they can (re)awaken spiritual hunger and thirst. Time in a prayer space can revive that 'initial natural capacity' for spirituality, no matter how it's been damaged or how long it's lain dormant (and this is just as true for adults as it is for children).

When Carole, the head of RE at a state secondary school in Suffolk, England, was asked about the impact of their first prayer space, she said something remarkable:

> I have been extremely moved, both by the comments pupils have written at the prayer activities and [by] the feedback they have given to me when they have returned to class. *It's as if the prayer space has tapped into a vein of spirituality in our pupils that none of us, themselves included, knew they had.* Even pupils who exhibit challenging behaviours in some lessons have been calm as soon as they walk into the space. Pupils who were already Christians seem relieved that their classmates now understand how faith helps them

> through their daily lives. And the SLT [Senior Leadership Team] have been delighted at how well it contributes to the spiritual development of the pupils. I have nothing but praise for the work of the team who set it up and the impact it has had on our school. (Emphasis added.)

In Eugene H. Peterson's poetic paraphrase of Matthew 5 in *The Message*, Jesus says, 'Let me tell you why you are here. You're here to be salt-seasoning that brings out the God-flavors of this earth . . . Here's another way to put it: You're here to be light, bringing out the God-colors in the world.'[8] When you host a prayer space in school, it's an opportunity to bring out the spiritual flavours and colours in each and every pupil's life, to affirm what the Holy Spirit has done, and is currently doing, in their lives and awaken the God-hunger and the God-thirst within them (even though they may not recognise that's what it is yet).

Researching Prayer

By the start of 2017, we'd heard hundreds of stories from prayer spaces in schools, but we still had lots of questions about what was actually taking place, and particularly about the ways that children and young people were expressing and exploring their spirituality through the prayer activities. So a friend suggested that I should go and talk with a professor about it.

I don't know why, but the first time I went to York to see Professor Julian Stern (at that time, Professor of Education and Religion at York St John University) I felt nervous. Maybe it was because it felt a little bit like going to see a school head teacher, and my distant memories of visiting head teachers' offices aren't ones I savour. Or maybe his name had subliminally affected me, and I was expecting someone 'stern' and disapproving? Anyway, Julian was the complete opposite of all that I feared. When I arrived at the university campus, he welcomed me warmly and invited me into his tiny office, immediately offering to make a cup of tea (like any good English person would). My eyes were drawn to his floor-to-ceiling, over-stuffed bookshelves and I noticed his name on quite a few of the spines. (When I checked online, I discovered that most of his books were listed as 'academic', so they were ridiculously expensive. I did manage to wangle a freebie off him a few months later though. Books are one of my love languages – just so you know.)

While Julian and I drank tea, he talked about his recent research into spirituality and solitude, which involved interviewing twelve- to thirteen-year-old pupils about their experiences of aloneness in school.

He told me about a girl called Gill who'd said, 'I wish there were more times when we could just relax and take all the stress away from our lives because sometimes it all gets built up inside me.' And about Eliza who'd agreed, adding, 'If my school had a quiet room, I would definitely spend time there.'[9] I was astonished. I knew that Julian was a professor of religion, but I had no idea that his research and his writing would be so similar to what we'd been doing with prayer spaces in schools, and so I told him some of our stories. And then, towards the end of our meeting, I made my pitch – I told Julian that we wanted someone to do some independent research, to evaluate the contribution that prayer spaces were making to children's and young people's spiritual development. To my delight, Julian agreed, and so we began making plans.

The research project turned out to involve a tremendous amount of work for all of us. We helped Julian and his co-researcher, Rachael Shillitoe, make contact with schools all over England that had recently hosted prayer spaces, and twenty-four of them agreed to participate. A total of 555 pupils from those schools completed a lengthy questionnaire regarding what they thought and felt about their experiences, and then Julian and Rachael visited seven of the schools, where they conducted eighty-six in-person interviews (mostly with pupils, but with a few staff too).

A few months after they'd completed the project, we invited Julian and Rachael to present their findings at one of our national conferences, where they showed slides filled with statistics and quotes from pupils and staff, and summarised the key themes. They explained that their findings echoed those of a previous study into children's spirituality conducted by David Hay and Rebecca Nye in 2006,[10] which described four areas of relational spirituality: me and myself, me and others, me and the world, and me and God/the 'Divine Other'. Julian and Rachael used this as the basis for their presentation, and it has informed how we have understood prayer spaces in schools ever since. (It has also helped me to understand and attend to my own spiritual journey, but that's another story.)

Reconciliation

If I were to summarise these four areas of relational spirituality in just one word it would be 'reconciliation', and it's the best word I can think of to describe the purpose of every prayer space too. We want to help children and young people to be:

- reconciled with themselves – by learning to love themselves as they are, uniquely made and valuable beyond measure;

Reconciliation

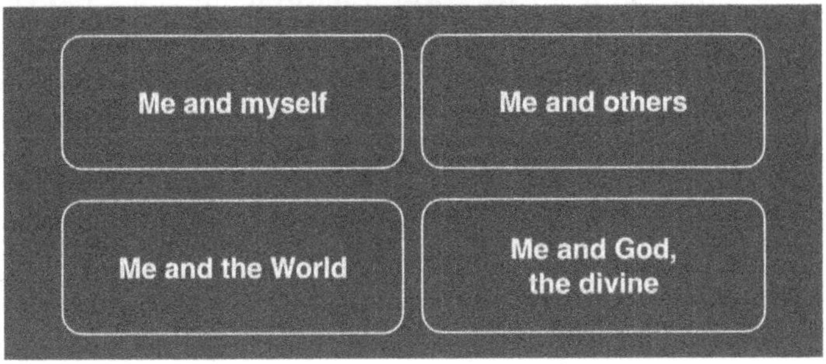

- reconciled with others – by learning to love others and make connections with them, through gratitude and encouragement, through forgiveness and through receiving forgiveness too;
- reconciled with the world around them – by learning how to be good stewards of the earth, and by learning how to act justly, love mercy and walk humbly;
- and reconciled with God – by learning how to receive God's love and know God personally.

Reconciliation, of course, is God's purpose for *all* things, as described in Paul's letter to the Colossian church: 'For God was pleased to have all his fullness dwell in him, *and through him to reconcile to himself all things, whether things on earth or things in heaven,* by making peace through his blood, shed on the cross'[11] (emphasis added). God's ultimate purpose for all things is reconciliation, restoration, relationship – it's God's mission.

However, we don't get to simply sit back and enjoy the ride while God does all the reconciling work. In his second letter to the Corinthian church, Paul writes, 'God . . . reconciled us to himself through Christ and *gave us the ministry of reconciliation*: that God was reconciling the world to himself in Christ, not counting people's sins against them. And he has committed to us the message of reconciliation. We are therefore Christ's ambassadors, as though God were making his appeal through us. We implore you on Christ's behalf: Be reconciled to God'[12] (emphasis added). God's ultimate purpose for all things is reconciliation, and God invites us to participate in this – reconciliation is our mission too.

So, what's the vision of prayer spaces in schools? What's the big idea? Put simply, it's reconciliation. It's about helping children and young people to love themselves, to love others, to love the world and everything in it, and to love God and be loved by God. Prayer spaces in schools aren't everything, by any stretch of the imagination, but they definitely contribute something – perhaps something important – to God's mission. Over the next few chapters, we're going to explore each of these four areas of reconciliation in turn by examining a few prayer activities that are linked to each theme and by hearing stories about the ways that children and young people have used them to explore and express their spiritual journeys.

Reflect and Pray

1. Rebecca Nye says that children have an 'initial natural capacity for awareness of the sacred quality to life experiences'. Can you recall a childhood memory that felt 'spiritual' in some way? Maybe it was a moment of wonder, of mystery or connectedness, of reconciliation, or something else.

2. Think of a young child whom you know. Maybe one within your family, or the child of a friend. Ask God to show you how you could be 'like salt, bringing out the God-flavors' or 'like light, bringing out the God-colors' in their life in some small way.

3. Thinking about the 'relational spirituality' framework, pause for a few moments to pray one thing for

yourself, one thing for a friend, and one thing for a situation that you are aware of in the world, and then listen for God to speak to you.

PRAYER ACTIVITY: RECONCILIATION ZIPS

Given that I've ended this chapter talking about reconciliation, it seems appropriate to include the details for Reconciliation Zips. This activity was designed by Jane Whittington, a head teacher who hosted one of the very first prayer spaces in her primary school.

What is it?

When people argue and fight, it's like they get separated from each other. They're not together any more. And it's not just individuals who get separated from each other. Whole groups of people can become separated because of their skin colour, their religious beliefs, their postcodes, their clothing styles . . . all kinds of things. When we allow these things to separate us, we forget that we are all human beings, and that we belong together.

This activity invites pupils to think about their own relationships, their friends or family, or even something that they are aware of around the world, where people have become separated. And then it invites them to express a hope, a wish or a prayer for reconciliation, for relationships to be restored, by using a simple zip.

How does it work?

All that you really need for this activity is a collection of zips. You can buy new ones (I got a pack of them online) or you can use ones from old clothing, as long as you make sure that they do up smoothly. It will help to have a table and chairs or cushions to create a comfortable area.

If appropriate, you can provide somewhere for the pupils to lay the zips. In a church school you could use a cross, or you might like them to lay their zips at the base of a globe if you are thinking of situations overseas.

Who is it for?

This works for children and young people of any age.

Instructions

When people argue and fight, they get separated from each other. They're not together any more. Have you argued with someone recently? Do you know people who don't get on well together?

Zips are clever. Zips bring two sides together. Reconciliation means bringing two sides together. Pick up a zip and think about the people you want to bring back together. If you want to, you can say a quiet prayer for the people you're thinking of as you do up the zip. This is a reconciliation prayer.

A little story . . .

At the end of a prayer space session with a group of twelve- to thirteen-year-olds, I asked the pupils to gather back together for a bit of feedback before the bell sounded for the end of the lesson. As soon as I asked the first question, 'What was your favourite prayer activity, and why?', a girl sitting directly in front of me put her hand up. 'The friendship activity,' she said, pointing to Reconciliation Zips on a table in the opposite corner. She turned and looked at the girl sitting next to her and they grinned at each other. 'We've been rowing (arguing) all week, but we used the zips and now we're mates again.'

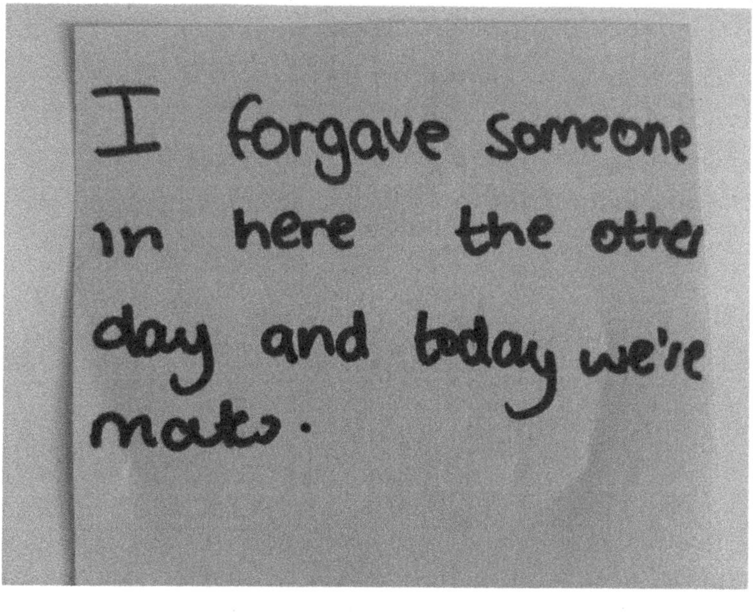

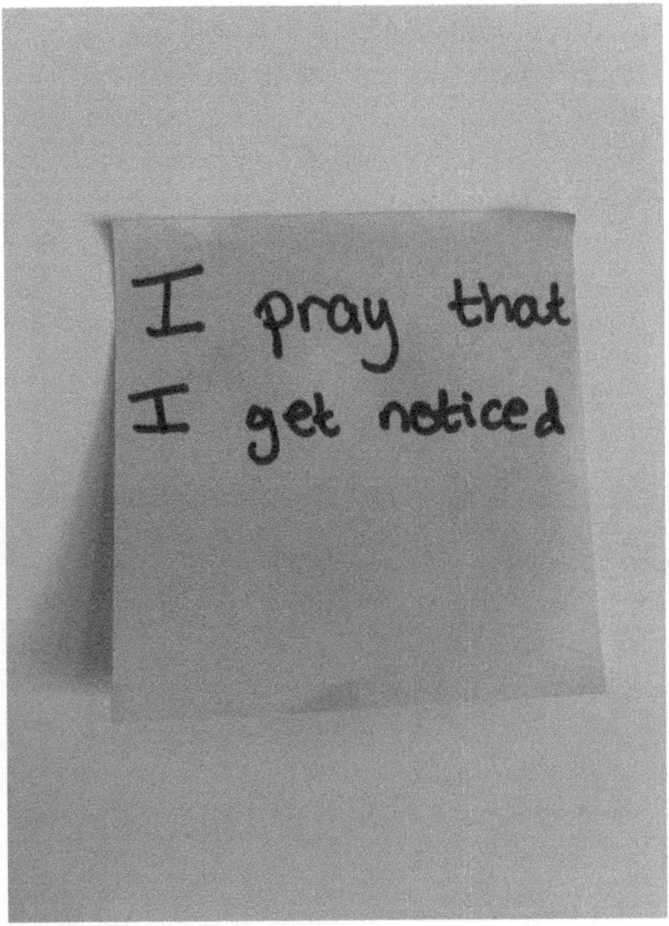
I pray that
I get noticed

5

Fearfully and Wonderfully Made[1]

Being reconciled with myself

What pupils say: *'I liked everything. It let me open myself and be me, not something that's not me.'*—Boy, aged thirteen

What teachers say: '*I can't believe how calm and peaceful they are. They were just crazy in the classroom. I was worried about bringing them in here.*'—Teacher, UK

* * *

Prayer spaces can help children and young people to become reconciled with themselves – to accept and love themselves a little bit more – in a culture that tells them that who they are and what they do is never quite enough. Children and young people are under constant pressure to be 'something that's not me' (to quote the boy who wrote the comment above), and this is one of the reasons behind the current crisis in children's and young people's mental health and wellbeing.

In England, in 2021 the National Health Service (NHS) said that '1 in 6 children aged 5–16 are identified as having a probable mental health problem'.[2] And it's even worse on the other side of the Atlantic Ocean, where, according to the US Department of Health and Human Services, '1 in 5 U.S. children ages 3–17 has a mental, emotional, behavioural, or developmental disorder'.[3] Just let these statistics sink in for a moment . . . that's between five and six children out of every classroom of thirty. If you're reading this and you're not from the UK or the USA, I'd encourage you to do some research about the statistics where you are.

There are many ways (some direct, some indirect) that prayer spaces can help pupils to love themselves a little bit more, but the three areas that I'm going to focus on are:

- Self-image
- Wellbeing (and being still)
- Creating safe spaces

Self-image

One of the simplest and maybe most effective prayer activities is called Mirrors (or Be Yourself). In recent years, prayer space practitioners have developed more complex versions of this activity involving multiple mirrors along a labyrinth-like route within a tent or gazebo, but the basic set-up requires one full-length mirror secured to a wall in a corner of a classroom, surrounded by positive, encouraging quotes.

Ruth, James and I used the Mirrors activity when we hosted our second prayer space in 2009. By then, schools were scheduling classes to visit the prayer space as part of their RE and PSHE (personal, social and health education) timetable, and at the end of one of the lessons, our friend Marcus was hosting a brief feedback session with the class. He asked which activities the twelve-year-old pupils liked the most, and lots of hands went up. 'The Prayer Wall . . . because I saw that other people feel the same as me.' 'The Be Sorry bin . . . because I had something I needed to get off my chest.' 'The Thankyou Card . . . because I never got to say thank you to my Grandad when he died.'

Then Marcus asked if there were any prayer activities that they *didn't* like (always risky), or maybe found difficult (slightly less risky), and a girl sitting on the floor in front of him slowly raised her hand. 'The one with the mirror,' she said, before hesitating for a moment, perhaps wondering whether it was safe to say more. 'I didn't like it,' she continued, 'because I didn't like what I saw.'

Marcus is a big-bearded, bald guy, and looking at him back then, you'd probably think that he had a Harley-Davidson motorcycle or something similar in the parking area outside. But Marcus is also one of the gentlest, most father-hearted men I know, and I think everyone experienced this as he smiled warmly. 'You heard me say at the start that I'm a Christian, right?' he said, looking around the class. 'Well, Christians believe that God made every single human being uniquely different but equally important. And Christians believe that when God was done, God looked at each human being, one by one, and went . . . "WOW! I did a great job!" And,' he said, looking back at the girl in front of him, 'if all that is true, then it goes for me, and I believe it goes for you too. All of the positive quotes you read around that mirror over there are true for all of us.' The girl smiled. It seemed like Marcus's words had got through.

* * *

Something similar happened when I was helping to host a prayer space in a secondary school in the north of England. A class of fifteen- to sixteen-year-olds came for their RE lesson early in the week. Stephen, the local youth worker, did a short introduction and then the pupils started drifting slowly from activity to activity.

There was a lot of laughing and chatting going on and the pupils weren't really engaging, except at the Mirrors activity, which Urszula, our 'team grandma', was looking after. (Trust me, every team needs a grandma!) I noticed that she was encouraging the pupils to use it in pairs – one in front of the mirror, with the other standing directly behind them, reading aloud the positive quotes that surrounded the mirror – and it seemed to be working well.

At the end of the lesson, Stephen gathered the pupils into a semicircle around him and asked for some feedback. At first the pupils just jostled one another and joked around, but eventually one of the boys spoke up. 'I've got something to say,' he said, shifting a little so that he could address his classmates. 'You think you know me because you know I'm good at sports and I do all right in school. But what you don't know about me is that when I look at myself in the mirror at home every morning, I . . . hate myself.' For a moment, it felt like no one dared breathe – you could've heard a proverbial pin drop. As I looked at the faces around the room, I realised that two very special things were taking place at that moment. First, just like the girl in Marcus's prayer space, this boy had made a brave decision – to trust that the prayer space was a safe place to be open about his suffering. And second, by being vulnerable himself, he was making it a safe place for others to do the same. And that's exactly what happened. For the rest of the week, pupils from this class came back during break times to talk with the team (mostly with Urszula).

* * *

When Ian and his team of volunteers set up their prayer space at a primary school in the south of England, they decided to adapt the Mirrors prayer activity. He wrote:

> One of the main themes for this prayer space was self image, so we set up some large mirrors with positive words around them. We asked the pupils to pick two words to describe themselves as they looked into the mirror. It soon became clear how difficult this task was for them, and so we asked them to choose words for a friend instead. They began encouraging their friends, which was amazing. And then a group of girls dragged their teacher over to the mirror and said, 'Miss, we think you're pretty and kind and really helpful.'
> 'Really? Do you think I'm pretty?' she replied. She seemed to grow taller before my eyes. It clearly meant a lot to her.

'I was bowled over,' Ian said when I spoke with him. 'The impact that these simple activities can have is astounding. When I asked the head teacher for some feedback a week later he said that the prayer space had been a success, but that the self-image activities had definitely had the greatest impact – in his words, it had "transformed the school" that week. He said he'd never experienced such a positive feel in the school before.'

Being Enough

Sadly, this 'positive feel' is something that children and young people don't experience very often. It's hard for them to feel good about themselves because consumer culture is constantly bombarding them with the opposite message – 'You are not OK. You are not . . . enough.' The way they look isn't attractive enough. What they eat and drink isn't healthy enough. What they wear isn't cool enough. What they're listening to or watching or who they're following on social media, or what they're saying or liking or not liking . . . none of it is enough. But that's the purpose, the very nature of consumer culture – to make children and young people feel dissatisfied enough with some aspect of their lives that they want/must have whatever the advertisers are offering.

The gap between the 'me' that children and young people really are and the 'me' that they must present on social media, as well as in person to their friends at school, is getting wider. This gap is a deadly, dark chasm, and it's where anxiety and loneliness and self-harm and all kinds of mental health problems lurk. According to research conducted by the Children's Society and the charity Young Minds, 'Thirty eight percent of young people reported that social media has a negative impact on how they feel about themselves. This was exacerbated for girls, with 46 per cent of them stating that social media had a negative impact on their self-esteem.'[4]

As I've already said, prayer spaces can't do everything. Many children and young people need therapy or counselling or some other professional support to deal with the negative things they feel about themselves and the way that this affects their daily lives. However, prayer spaces clearly can do something good. Prayer activities like Mirrors seem to help some children and young people begin to see themselves in a more positive way, and hopefully love themselves a little bit more. They also provide safe places for healthy conversations around self-image and identity. And here's the really exciting bit: prayer spaces are places of encounter with the Holy Spirit, the One who can bring peace and healing and real transformation.

'I sort of feel like . . . it made me feel like . . . whole. It filled in the gaps.'—Boy, aged twelve

Wellbeing

Conversations about wellbeing have increased over the last few years, in the UK and in other nations too, and a brief bit of book-browsing or Google-searching will offer a multitude of slightly different definitions of the word.

On one of the UK government's websites, a paper by the Childhood Wellbeing Research Centre describes wellbeing as 'a dynamic state that is enhanced when people can fulfil their personal and social goals and achieve a sense of purpose in society. Rather than being static, wellbeing emerges from how people interact with the world around them at different points in their lives. It is not necessarily the same as being happy, since anxiety, depression and anger are sometimes to be expected in life.'[5] The Children's Society puts it a little more succinctly: 'Wellbeing is about how we are doing and how we feel about our lives.'[6]

You can download apps to help with your wellbeing, most of which will offer various techniques and exercises to build into your daily routines. Many workplaces now have wellbeing and mental health guidelines for their employees, which line managers are expected to use when they check in with their staff. And then there are all sorts of programmes being developed for schools too, because teachers recognise that pupils are generally not doing well, especially since the Covid-19 pandemic. The National Center for Education Statistics, for example, identified that: 'As of April 2022–about 2 years after the onset of the coronavirus pandemic in the United States–69 percent of public schools reported an increase in mental health concerns among their students.'[7]

Prayer spaces aren't specifically designed to be wellbeing projects, of course, but school staff often comment on the important contribution that they make. When the Head of Education for South Ayrshire in Scotland visited his first prayer space, he emailed the following feedback to us:

> 'The prayer spaces I have seen make a very effective contribution, not only to religious education, but also to health and wellbeing outcomes. They are well thought out and encourage children and young people to stop and think. In a world of constant stimulation, the time for reflection may be helpful for children's and young people's emotional wellbeing.

Being Still

One of the simplest ways, and possibly the most significant, that a prayer space can contribute to a pupil's wellbeing is by offering a place and time to pause and be still. For example, a volunteer from a local church emailed to tell us about the first prayer space that she helped to set up in a primary school:

> We set up the Be Still activity – we called it our Calm Tent – and a Year 2 [aged 6–7] class came in at the start of the day. The Teaching Assistant [TA] took me aside and said, 'I'm not sure how Kyle is going to behave as he is not having a good day.' This little boy struggled with ADHD and behavioural issues, and as soon as the session started, he went and sat in the Calm Tent. He shook the calm jars that we'd created, and he listened to the iPod narration over and over again, and so the TA and I decided to leave him to it as he seemed to be pretty happy. At the end of the day, we were packing up when the TA came back to the prayer space to talk with me. 'It's been amazing,' she said. 'Kyle has had such a good day after being in the Calm Tent this morning. It's like he's a different child.'

Before we hosted our first prayer spaces in a school, if you'd asked me which would be the most popular prayer activity, I would've put Be Still close to the bottom of the list because, well, there's nothing to do in it. The activity simply invites pupils to sit or lie down and try their best to *not* do anything. I was convinced that other activities would be more popular because children and young people need to be entertained . . . right? They need to be occupied and amused, which is why we constantly need to innovate and make things new and interesting, or else they'll get bored . . . right?

As it turns out . . . wrong. When Ruth, James and I asked the pupils who had participated in our first prayer space for their favourite prayer activity, the majority said or pointed to the Be Still tent (which is doubly surprising, given that ours kept falling down). And for the last fifteen years, with very few exceptions, pupils have consistently said the same thing about every prayer space. The only conclusion I can come to is that children and young people crave stillness. They just don't know how to do it. No one has shown them *how* to be still.

After visiting people all over the world who were experimenting with slower ways to live and work and raise their families, the Canadian journalist and author Carl Honoré concluded that human beings desperately need to 'make time for activities that defy acceleration'.[8] Life is getting faster all the time. We're constantly trying to do more, achieve more, fit more in, never stopping to breathe, and this relentless pursuit of more-of-everything is really, *really* not good for us.

In schools all over the UK, and in other places around the world, children and young people are entering school classrooms that have been temporarily transformed into prayer spaces to do the very same thing – to defy acceleration, to be still, and for many, to pray. Here are some of the things that pupils say about their experience:

'Everything is very busy. Good to have time to myself, to be quiet and think.'

'Be Still really helped me calm down a lot as I am hyper.'

'Before I went in I felt weary, but after I felt a lot happier.'

'When I went in I just felt relaxed and refreshed. Before I had felt worried.'

'Thank you so much for letting me think about everything that's happened and relieving stress as it's hard to do so elsewhere.'

'In the Be Still tent the lava lamp reminded me of all the things in my head and how they all move around and sometimes need to stop.'

'I liked expressing my feelings and relaxing my anger and sadness. I feel I can never do it at home because

I can never be alone and express myself. But I still pray.'

* * *

A few years ago, some of the Anglican Diocese of Durham's five secondary schools decided to run prayer spaces during the same month. I ran workshops for groups of older pupils from each school, teaching them how to design their own prayer activities (see Chapter 9). And then, when it was time to run the prayer spaces, the pupils visited each other's schools to collaborate and evaluate them together. It was a huge success. Afterwards, Gill Booth, the executive head teacher of two of the schools, was amazed at the feedback she'd received, both from pupils and from staff in all of the schools. 'The activities gave pupils an opportunity to explore faith, whether they had a personal faith or not. Both pupils and staff enjoyed the experience, with many choosing to revisit the prayer space during lunchtimes and after school. Nothing we've done has had a greater impact on our pupils' wellbeing,' she concluded.

Creating Safe Spaces

For many children and young people, the world simply doesn't feel safe, either because of what they see and hear on social media, or because of what they experience at home or in their schools. And because everything feels like a threat, children and young people find themselves unable to respond, except to 'fight, flight, freeze or fawn'. To help children and young people not to feel anxious, 'we need to create circumstances and spaces . . . safe spaces where they can be themselves'.[9]

When Ben and the Scripture Union (SU) team realised that their upcoming prayer space in a secondary school was going to coincide with the Olympic Games, they decided to use this as the overall theme. They set up the classroom with ribbons and national flags, and included prayer activities such as Weightlifting Worries, Football Prayers and The Olympic Flame. Ben was delighted when the school's PE department let him borrow an athletics hurdle because it meant that they could also set up a visual prayer activity called Overcoming Hurdles. Some prayer activities, such as Be Still, can take quite a bit of preparation, but this one is really simple. All it takes is some pieces of string tied to a hurdle so that they dangle down, and then some torn-up cardboard, felt-tip pens and clothes pegs so that pupils can write their prayers and then peg them to the string. That's it – easy-peasy.

Given my limited experience of hurdling, I was surprised to discover that Olympic sprint hurdles are set at 106.7 cm for men and 83.8 cm for women. If you can, pause for a moment to measure how high up your body this comes, because I'm sure you'll agree that it's ridiculous. Olympic hurdles are not easy to jump over, which brings us to the point of the activity: there are lots of things in our lives that we find hard to get over, or to get past.

Once Ben had positioned the hurdle in the corner of the classroom, he printed out the following simple instructions to go with it:

> What are the hurdles in your life? What are the things that you're finding difficult to get over or get past? If you want to, you can write or draw about this on one of the pieces of cardboard and then peg it to the strings. And if you want to, as you do it, you can ask for God's help.

One of the groups that visited this Olympic-themed prayer space was a class of thirteen-year-olds. As usual, Ben introduced his team to the pupils and explained each of the prayer activities, and then he gave them thirty to forty minutes to explore the space. They quickly spread out around the room – some in small groups and others on their own – and they soon quietened down and began to try the activities. After a few minutes, Ben noticed a boy standing alone beside the hurdle. He seemed upset, so Ben discreetly pointed him out to the class teacher, who went over to check if he was OK. They talked for a couple of minutes before the boy asked if he could leave the classroom for a while.

Later that night, my friend Lucy called to say that her nephew had visited a prayer space at his school, and did I know anything about it? When I said yes, she told me this extraordinary story: 'My sister adopted Danny when he was three years old, so he was old enough to know what was happening to him and to be affected by it. But Danny never really talked about his feelings, and especially about being adopted. Not until last night, anyway. When he came home from school, he told my sister – his mum – all about the prayer space, and then he described the hurdles activity and he said that it kind of opened up something inside of him that he didn't really know what to do about. And then Danny started talking about how he felt – something he's not done in ten years – about being adopted, and how he thinks this has made it a bit difficult for him to trust people and make friends. He said, "I feel like there's a big hole inside me." He's asking for help, and I think he knows he needs God's help too.'

I told Lucy that the prayer space would be there all week, and that Ben was working as a part-time chaplain in the school, so he'd be there after the prayer space was packed away, and if Danny ever wanted someone else to talk with, Ben would be available.

* * *

It was Friday lunchtime, and Sam, a local youth worker, and I were sitting on one of the desks in a corner of the prayer space at his school. We noticed a boy – probably around fourteen years old – sitting across the room, eating his lunch and watching other pupils use the prayer activities. Eventually, he came over, but when he spoke his voice was so quiet that I could barely hear him. 'I want to write a sorry prayer,' he whispered to Sam, 'but I want you to see it.'

For the Be Sorry activity, Sam and his team had tied lengths of string to the classroom ceiling above a desk on which there was a pile of torn-up cardboard and some felt-tip pens. Pupils had been writing their sorry prayers onto the cardboard and either pegging them onto the strings or just piling them on the table. The boy glanced at Sam and then picked up a pen and a piece of cardboard. From where I was sitting, it looked like he took a deep breath before writing something, and then he hid his cardboard prayer among the others on the table. Sam and the boy stood in silence for a couple of minutes and then Sam guided him across to a couple of chairs, where they talked for a little while.

Later that afternoon, Sam told me the story: 'He wrote, "I hate my life. I'm sorry for wanting to end it all" on the cardboard. He's been in the prayer space every break time, just sitting there, eating his packed lunch. I've said hello a few times, but he never seemed to want to talk, and then he goes and writes this! You know, I think he spent the whole week figuring out if the prayer space was a safe place, and probably if we were safe people too.'

Sam's story isn't unusual in the sense that, for many young people, prayer spaces have become safe places, safe havens, an oasis in their daily desert. Coincidentally, as I write this chapter, plans are under way to develop prayer spaces in the Czech Republic, and they have decided to call them *oáza*, which means 'oasis'.

Keeping Prayer Spaces Safe: A Few Practical Reflections

Prayer spaces are places where children and young people have the potential to be or feel vulnerable, either because of the thoughts or feelings that they may be processing internally, or because there are adults in the room whom they may not know well. Therefore, when planning your prayer space, you need to:

1. Talk with whoever is responsible for safeguarding in the school (if that role exists). In British and American schools they are usually called the Designated Safeguarding Lead, or DSL. In other nations they may be called the Child Protection Lead/Child Protection Officer or something similar. Ask about the school's safeguarding policies and practices.
2. Recruit your team carefully. You are responsible for ensuring that whoever is hosting the prayer space is safe to work with pupils in school. There will probably be some safety checks that you need to make.
3. Train your team well. Get some safeguarding training yourself, and then ensure that your team knows how to identify concerns and how to respond.

We've developed some general principles to help people ensure that their prayer spaces are safe places, and we encourage anyone hosting prayer spaces to download these and adapt them. Although safeguarding policies and practices differ greatly from nation to nation, the general principles we've developed are probably useful anywhere. You can find them on our websites, but here are a few of the main points to give you an idea of what safe working looks like:

A Few Tips for Keeping Your Prayer Space Safe . . .

- Work in pairs at the very least. There should be a minimum of two people, ideally at least one of each sex, hosting the prayer space whenever there are pupils present. Never be on your own with a child or a young person where you can't be observed.

- Work appropriately. Avoid any contact with pupils which is, or could be interpreted as being, inappropriate, sexual or violent (words, threats, jokes, actions).

- Say something. Do not take concerns out of the school. If you are told about a situation of abuse, or neglect, or anything illegal or potentially harmful, you must pass this information on to a teacher (unless they are the cause of your concern) or go straight to whoever is responsible for safeguarding in the school. You should also make your own notes about the conversation before leaving the school, and a copy should be left with the school. (Hopefully, the school will have a specific form for this.)

- Confidentiality. Don't promise confidentiality if a pupil tells you anything about neglect or abuse. If a child or a young person wants to talk to you, listen, but don't investigate or ask leading questions. Let the pupil know that you will need to tell a teacher about your conversation. Assure them that they are not to blame and that they have done the right thing by telling you. Once again, make your own notes.

- Contact details. Do not accept contact details from any pupil or give contact details to any pupil, or make contact with them through social media, even after the prayer space has finished.

- Do something. If you have a concern, act on it. You might be the first person to realise there is reason to be concerned about a pupil. Don't assume that someone else already knows or will notice later. Don't walk out of the school knowing something of concern that you have not passed on.

Reflect and Pray

1. Find a mirror – preferably a full-length one – and take a good look at yourself. What do you think, and how do you feel, about who you see? Talk with God about this.

2. Carl Honoré says that we need to 'make time for activities that defy acceleration'. How could you do that sometime over the next couple of days? Where could you go to simply sit and be still for a few minutes? (Turn your devices off or, better still, leave them behind while you go to your quiet place.)

3. What could your church community do to create safer spaces for children and young people?

PRAYER ACTIVITY: BE STILL (AKA THE BOUNCY CASTLE – SEE PAGE 54)

Almost every prayer space includes some kind of Be Still prayer activity.

What is it?

Schools are busy places. In fact, our whole lives are busy, full of noise and other people and things to do and places we should be. We rarely get to stop, to switch off, and just be. But as someone once pointed out, we are called human beings and not human doings. This activity encourages pupils to pause and be still for a few minutes, to be silent and listen.

How does it work?

The easiest way to set up this activity is to use a gazebo frame or child's pop-up tent, and fill it with some bean bags or floor cushions. You could also include some subtle lighting, battery-powered candles and/or a lava lamp to add a bit of atmosphere, and some laminated quotes about being still or peaceful. Try not to fill the emptiness too much though – empty space, after all, is an important part of this prayer activity.

If you don't have a gazebo, use some drapes or sheets to create a space which is almost enclosed, allowing those inside some privacy. Make sure that the entrance can't be closed completely, to discourage inappropriate behaviour and ensure that the pupils inside are safe.

Who is it for?

Anyone! Pupils of all ages. School staff. Volunteers before and after the prayer space starts. Caretakers and cleaning staff who might want to sneak in during the evenings.

Any other information?

A Be Still space works best when you limit the number of pupils – two or three at a time is probably best. You may need to introduce a time limit of two or three minutes to ensure that all the pupils who want to use the activity can do so.

Instructions

The word 'holy' simply means 'set apart'. For hundreds of years, people have discovered that being set apart from other people helps them to be more aware of themselves and also more aware of God. In our busy world, this isn't easy. The Be Still space is just that – a place to be still. It is a holy space. There is no need to talk, no need to do anything. Just be.
'Be still, and know that I am God.' (Psalm 46:10).

A little story . . .

A Muslim girl in a local community primary school asked if she could use the Be Still tent one lunchtime. She explained that all her friends were having lunch, and she didn't really want to be with them because it was Ramadan and she was fasting. She ended up staying for the whole hour, just lying on her back in the tent, looking at the lava lamp and the luminous stars that were stuck to the ceiling. When the bell eventually rang for the end of the lunch break, she said, 'I had no idea what this was going to be like, but it's absolutely amazing. I'd love to be here all the time. I didn't feel alone.'

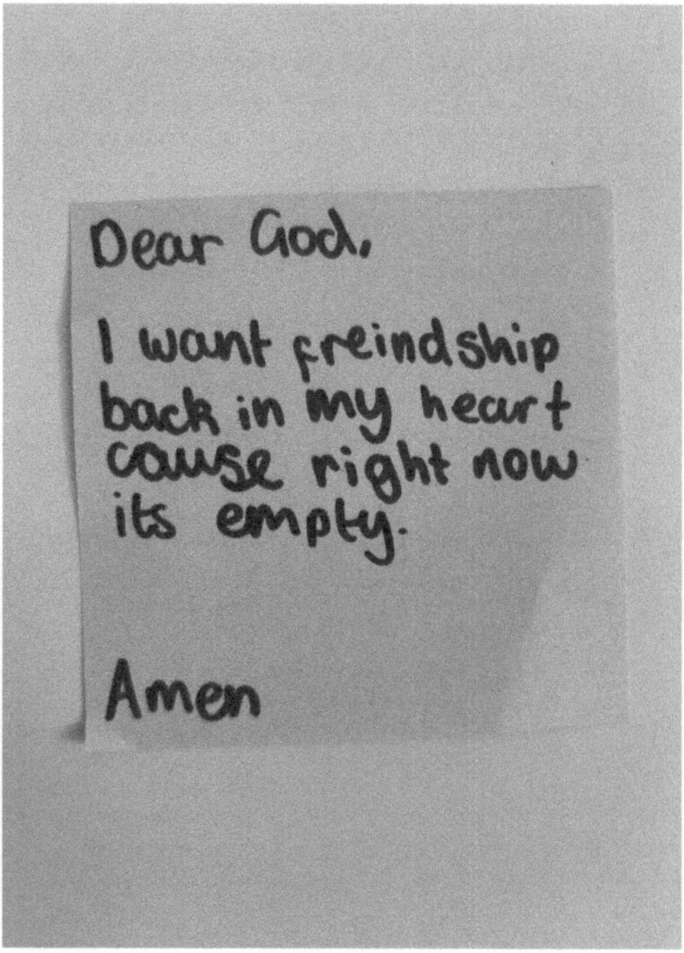
Dear God,
I want freindship
back in my heart
cause right now
its empty.
Amen

6

Let Us Love One Another[1]

Being reconciled with others

What pupils say: *'Nothing in the world can break forgiveness.'*—Girl, aged ten

What school chaplains say: '*An amazing week was had with lots of tears, honest reflection and plenty of forgiveness.*'—Secondary school chaplain, UK

* * *

Prayer spaces can help children and young people to be reconciled with others – to love other people a little bit more – in a culture that is increasingly divided and fearful of anyone who appears to be different or 'other', and one in which people are quick to cancel others instead of making any attempt to resolve relational conflict. Recent research reveals that despite the many digital connections children and young people have, they are increasingly lonely, isolated and fearful of other people.

Many of the activities in our online resource libraries are themed around relationships, and they aim to help children and young people love one another just a little bit more. The three areas that I'm going to focus on in this chapter are:

- Friendship
- Forgiveness
- Grief and loss

Friendship

The introduction to the Friendship (or Character Cards) prayer activity says:

> Children and young people often find it hard to see and speak good things about one another, and they find it even harder to see and speak good things about themselves. It's always easier to see and say bad things, negative things. (Adults aren't very different.) Sometimes we need a friend to help us see the good things about ourselves. This activity encourages pupils to identify and affirm positive characteristics that they see in each other, to see and speak good things, to encourage each other.

For this activity all you really need is a table for two pupils to sit at (opposite each other is best), and a set of twenty cards with positive characteristics written on them – things like joy, kindness, trust, responsibility, hope, peace, inspiration, gratitude, courage, communication, and so on. The two pupils each choose a couple of the positive characteristics that they see in each other, and then a prayer space host usually helps them to have a conversation about the words they've chosen by asking things like:

- Why did you choose this card?
- When have you seen them behaving this way?
- Have you ever told them they are like this?
- How much does this description match what you think of yourself?
- How does it feel knowing that someone else sees this as true of you?
- What words do you most like people to use when they describe you?

This activity is sometimes amusing, but it's always affirming and uplifting. At the end of his visit to a prayer space, one ten-year-old boy said, 'I think the most important activity was the Character Cards one because it made you realise what good friends you have got.

Also, when you picked out the words to describe them, it made you and them feel special.'

Character Cards can sometimes foster moments of profound reconciliation, as Tim recalled:

> In one of our prayer spaces in a secondary school a thirteen-year-old boy was bouncing around the room, going from one prayer activity to the next, hardly paying attention, and being something of a distraction to others. The previous week the class teacher had sent him out of the class because his behaviour was too disruptive to allow him to stay, and now his behaviour was further fuelled by his anger at what had happened a week ago. The teacher invited the boy to join him for the Character Cards activity, and so they sat down to each choose their two positive words. One of my team gently guided them through a conversation about the words they'd chosen and why, and as they did, the boy's body language changed visibly. From being tense, agitated and on the edge of his seat, he gradually started to relax as his teacher spoke words of affirmation over him, naming the positive aspects of his character. In turn, the boy told the teacher about the things he valued in him. It's difficult to convey the extraordinary change in this boy, but in just a few minutes his whole demeanour was

> transformed as he and the teacher were reconciled. For the second part of the lesson he was calm, engaging thoughtfully and respectfully with the other prayer activities around the room. He even said thank you as he left.

Some of the prayer activities in our online resource libraries are designed for pupils to do on their own. Most of these involve short narrations recorded on an MP3 player, which a child or young person can listen to through headphones, thus creating a bit of private space in an otherwise busy classroom. Mirrors (or Be Yourself) is usually a solitary activity too, although, as you read in the previous chapter, it can be quite effective when two friends use it together.

However, most of the activities in our online resource libraries are public in the sense that pupils use them alongside, or with, friends and classmates. Although there is something personal – private even – about reflection and prayer, there is also something communal about it. Children and young people draw strength and comfort from realising that others feel the same way they do – that others have similar worries, struggles, questions and hopes. This is one of the reasons why it is important to leave enough time at the end of a prayer space session to gather the pupils back together to reflect and try to make sense of what they've experienced. It's important that the pupils get to hear each other, because this often helps them to understand and articulate what they think and feel too.

On one occasion, due to a timetabling error, we ended up with two whole classes of fifteen-year-old pupils at one prayer space session in a local high school. We were in a pretty big science room, but even so, with nearly sixty teenagers in the room, it felt crowded. Large groups shuffled between the activities and pupils waited impatiently for their turn. Towards the end of the session, in a rather louder voice than usual, I asked the pupils to gather back together for some feedback, and they slowly spread around the room to find a bit of space, some sitting on desks and even window ledges. When I asked them how they felt about the prayer space, a girl in the far corner of the room stuck her hand up and said, 'It felt weird.' She frowned, adding, 'I think I felt a bit depressed actually.' I didn't really know how to respond to that, so I was grateful when another girl on the opposite side of the classroom interrupted. 'I know what you mean,' she said, 'but I didn't feel depressed. It was more like . . . this is going to sound a bit crazy because I know it's just a science classroom, but I felt like this room was *clean*, and I felt like I was, you know, *not* clean.' At which point, the first girl pointed across the room towards the second girl and almost shouted, 'Yes! That's it. I didn't feel depressed – I felt like what you said.' For a couple of minutes the room was silent as I explained how we can respond to feelings like these, feelings of guilt and shame, and how we can make positive choices and changes in our lives. I've rarely witnessed the gentle conviction of the Holy Spirit at work in such a beautiful way.

Our spiritual journeys are not solitary adventures. We are meant to walk with others. We were made for friendship, fellowship and companionship.[2] We disciple one another as we learn with and from one another and as we encourage one another. Incidentally, in the New Testament, the phrase 'one another' is derived from the Greek word *allelon*, which means 'one another, each other; mutually, reciprocally', and it appears around 100 times. Fifty-nine of these occurrences are specific commands which are meant to teach us how (and how not) to relate to one another, including things like 'serve one another',[3] 'spur one another on towards love and good deeds',[4] 'don't grumble against one another',[5] 'be patient, bearing with one another in love',[6] and many (many!) more. We were made for sharing life together, for relationships.

One of my favourite little stories is about a brother and sister who had both experienced the prayer space in their school. We received an email from their mum, and this is what she said:

> Jonathan has autism and life is challenging. A few weeks ago, his class had a prayer space and he loved it. Shortly afterwards, he started getting stressed about some things at school, and to my surprise Jonathan and his sister decided to make their own prayer space at home. It's been amazing and he has been completely calm all weekend. We just wanted to say thank you.

Forgiveness

I've sometimes wondered if my wife and I were better at encouraging our daughters to say 'I'm sorry' than 'I forgive you' while they were growing up. Both are important in the process of restoring relationships when things go wrong, but maybe 'I forgive you' is actually more important. It's certainly more difficult.

Interestingly, one of the most popular prayer activities is called Forgiveness Stones. It's one of a few that seem to work better when you record the script on an audio player and then invite pupils to sit down and listen to it through some headphones instead of reading it. (By the way, if you do this, use 'can'-style headphones and not earbuds – no one wants to use earbuds that someone else has used.) As I mentioned earlier, this creates a bit of privacy and helps the pupils to really focus on what they are doing.

The Forgiveness Stones narration begins by acknowledging that 'relationships can be fragile. Just as we all have the capacity for great acts of love and kindness, so too we all have the capacity to cause pain and sadness.' And then it asks a couple of questions: 'What hurtful things have you said or done to others? Other people can hurt us by the things they say and do. What hurt or painful memory are you carrying because of something said or done to you?'

In front of the pupil, there will be a small pile of fist-sized stones – these need to feel heavy – and a large bowl of clean water. As the narration continues, the pupil is invited to hold on to one of the stones. 'Let the stone represent the pain you feel when you remember what the other person said or did – you will probably have strong feelings: anger, sadness, a heavy heart. You may long for justice or even revenge. Think about what these feelings do to you. The other person may not know or care how you feel – they may never say sorry. We can't always see justice done, but we can be set free from the hurts.'

Finally, the narrator asks the pupil how they want to respond. 'Do you want to take these feelings with you?

Or would you rather let them go? To choose to let go of the hurts is to forgive. Jesus said, "If you forgive someone's sins, they're gone for good. If you don't forgive sins, what are you going to do with them?"[7] What will you do with your hurts? If you don't feel you can let them go just yet, put the stone back. If you have chosen to let the hurts go, place the stone into the bowl of water. Watch the water cover it. Remind yourself that you have chosen to let go. You may need to remember this in the days ahead. Know that as you forgive, so you also are forgiven.'

'The Forgiveness Stones activity always has a big impact,' said Sam, as we reflected on some of the prayer spaces that we'd both been involved with. 'I once asked a boy what he'd enjoyed in the prayer space and he said the Forgiveness Stones activity. "I really didn't want to forgive," he confessed, "but then I felt the weight of the stone in my hand and I realised that this is what I was carrying around inside me. I decided I didn't want to hold on to it any more, so I let it go, and I felt much better afterwards!" Isn't that amazing?'

As Sam told me that story, I remembered one of my own. I'd been sitting beside a seventeen-year-old girl as she carefully placed her stone into the bowl of water. After pausing for a moment, she took off the headphones, which was when I noticed the tears falling down her face. But then she smiled and said, 'It's taken me two years to let go of that!'

'To forgive,' wrote Lewis B. Smedes, 'is to set a prisoner free and discover that the prisoner was you.'[8]

Pupils sometimes use the Fizzy Forgiveness activity to say sorry, even though, like the Forgiveness Stones, it is really meant to be a 'forgiveness' activity (the clue is in the name). After one sixteen-year-old six-foot-tall rugby player had dropped his effervescent vitamin C tablet into the vase of water, he said, 'I felt like I couldn't let it go! I had to force myself to do it, and when I did, I immediately felt lighter.' He seemed genuinely surprised by what he'd experienced.

* * *

A few years ago, I received an email from a French missionary who was working in the jungles of the Democratic Republic of the Congo (DRC). She wanted to set up a prayer space for the abandoned girls she was working with. 'But I don't have a bubble tube, and I don't have a pop-up tent,' she wrote. 'What can I do?' We managed to schedule a video call while she was in one of the major cities and had access to decent Wi-Fi, and we came up with a plan together. Weeks later, it was amazing to see photos of the prayer space she constructed in what can only be described as a large shed with just some plastic chairs, some paper and pencils, and lots of jungle foliage!

The missionary sent me the most extraordinary email afterwards:

> We had an amazing week. One of the activities was to pray for those who need help and to my surprise most of these abandoned girls prayed for the parents who had abandoned them – for me it was a good lesson in forgiveness. God's love reaches the hearts of his children who have been hurt and gives them the strength and love to forgive like him. I was humbled.

Forgiving Myself

Sometimes the one the child or young person needs to forgive is themselves. The very first sticky note I picked up in my first prayer space is an example of this – '*There are so many things I can't forgive myself for. Can you forgive me God?'* My friend Joe sent me an email with another:

> The issue of forgiveness is so huge for young people. The main highlight of our prayer space week was a conversation I had with an 11 year old boy, originally from Argentina. He came over to the forgiveness activity – we had a whiteboard that pupils could write onto and then 'wipe the slate clean' – and he said to me, 'I did something really bad to my Grandad before he died', and then he burst into tears! It turns out that the last words he'd said to his Grandad before he'd died were, 'I hate you', and he felt terribly guilty. He said he didn't know why he'd said it, because he loved his Grandad, but he'd been carrying the pain of this moment for five years! I asked him to tell me some good stories about his Grandad, about the fun they'd had, and he seemed to cheer up. Eventually, I suggested that he could write the bad memory onto the whiteboard, and then wipe it away again as a way of saying sorry and letting go. I explained that I believe God forgives us, and that he should forgive himself too. Then I encouraged him to remember the good times he'd shared with his Grandad instead. And so he did it – he was so brave. He carries a

picture of his Grandad in his pocket, which he showed to me. He seemed a lot brighter and lighter when he left the prayer space.

Forgiveness Gives Life

Forgiveness is difficult, but studies have shown that it is actually good for human beings to forgive, and to receive forgiveness. 'Practising forgiveness can have powerful health benefits,' writes Dr Tyler VanderWeele of Harvard University. 'Observational studies, and even some randomised trials, suggest that forgiveness is associated with lower levels of depression, anxiety, and hostility; reduced substance abuse; higher self-esteem; and greater life satisfaction.'[9] Forgiveness isn't easy, but it can actually give us life.

Perhaps that's why Jesus talks very specifically about forgiveness, including it in the prayer that he taught his disciples, and then explaining it in greater depth immediately afterwards.[10] And then, when Peter asked if he should forgive someone seven times, Jesus said something truly outrageous: 'I tell you, not seven times, but seventy-seven times.'[11] Some versions translate this as 'seventy times seven times', but just in case someone you know is nearing their 490th offence, what Jesus actually means is, 'I tell you . . . keep forgiving, endlessly.'

'The most important activity for me was the forgiveness one,' wrote a ten-year-old boy on his feedback sheet. 'I felt this activity really gave me a chance to be forgiven and to forgive people. As I watched the tablet disappear, all my negative emotions fizzed away with it and now I feel as though I have really forgiven them.'

Grief and Loss

When the vicar of St George's Church, Adrian Hughes, heard that Andy, a popular thirteen-year-old boy in his parish, had suddenly died after a short battle with cancer, he wanted to do something to support Andy's parents, his friends, and the wider school community. So, early one evening he knocked on Andy's parents' door and simply asked them, 'What can I do to help?' Although they weren't Christians, they asked Adrian if he could host a memorial service at St George's, and after talking with the head teacher, they decided to open it up to the whole school community. Many came, including a lot of pupils.

While Adrian was wondering what they could do to further help the pupils with their grief, he heard that I was running a nearby workshop about prayer spaces in schools. His whole team from St George's showed up, and as soon as the session started Adrian knew that they'd found what they were looking for. Just a few weeks later, they set up their very first prayer space, including one very special prayer activity, The Empty Chair.

As I sat with Adrian in a coffee shop a few months later, reflecting on his memories of the prayer space, he said, 'We took a beautiful rocking chair from the vicarage and we placed it in one of the corners of the room and then spread cushions on the floor for the pupils to sit or kneel on. Then we invited the pupils to write their memories and prayers onto some luggage tags and tie them onto the chair. I think we expected to see lots of "RIP Andy" tags.' Adrian paused and smiled faintly before saying, 'Leaders are often naive in their expectations.

'We were so surprised by the detail with which some of the pupils wrote, and by the sheer number of tags too!' he said. 'By the end of the week it was almost impossible to see the rocking chair beneath the hundreds of luggage tags. And not just about Andy – pupils expressed their pain and suffering about friends they'd lost, pets who'd died, parents who'd separated, relatives they hadn't seen for many years.' Adrian said that they'd realised two very important things that week: first, that loss and grief are felt by children and young people more commonly than we might assume. And second, that children and young people are capable of expressing how they feel. They just don't usually have the time and safe places to do so.

At the end of the prayer space week, Adrian asked his team to help him load the rocking chair into his Skoda Octavia hatchback car. As they manoeuvred it through the corridors to the school car park, a couple of teachers asked what they were doing. They were visibly moved when Adrian explained, 'We're taking it to Andy's mum's house.'

'It felt strangely holy,' he reflected in the coffee shop. 'When I offered to bring the rocking chair round, she was very keen to see it,' Adrian continued. 'We edged it through her narrow front door and lowered it onto the carpet in the centre of their living room. Andy's mum, his brother and his sister began to read the luggage tags. We laughed together as she read and remembered some of Andy's funnier moments. And we wept together too.

'But Andy's legacy lives on,' Adrian smiled. 'The prayer space, and in particular, the introduction of The Empty Chair, was a parting gift. His death gave so many others an opportunity to process their grief and loss. I took the rocking chair to church on Sunday morning and explained what had happened in the prayer space and at Andy's family's house that week, and I invited the people in the service to come and read the luggage tags afterwards. I also left some blank ones beside the chair, just in case anyone wanted to add their own thoughts/prayers, and many did.'

'"Blessed are those who mourn,"' he said slowly, smiling again, '"for they will be comforted."'[12]

Hannah was the chaplain at a state primary school just north of Wellington in New Zealand. She'd been hosting prayer spaces called *Kia Inoi Tātou*[13] for a couple of years when tragedy struck. Just before a new term started, she heard that the popular deputy principal had died. It was completely unexpected and the whole school community was devastated. On the first day back, one of the other teachers stuck a sticky note expressing her sadness onto the deputy principal's office door. By the end of the day, there were a few other sticky notes with words of grief and gratitude and prayers for his family. By the end of the week, his door was completely covered. The school community had learned the language of reflection and prayer in the *Kia Inoi Tātou* prayer spaces.

It's OK To Not Be OK

Death is still a bit of a taboo subject. We don't know where and when we can talk about it. We're even a little bit scared of the word itself, and so we talk about people being 'no longer with us' or 'passing away' instead. And for children and young people, home isn't always a place where they can process what they think and how they feel when someone dies, sometimes because they see their mum or dad suffering too, and they don't want to add to their pain. And so they hold it all in.

In his research summary, Julian Stern observed that pupils frequently used their time in prayer spaces to process grief and loss, whether that was to do with a friend or a family member who had died, or occasionally a pet. (I have to confess, I wasn't very sympathetic towards people who got terribly upset when their pets died . . . until we got two dogs of our own, and now I'm desperately hoping that they'll live forever.)

Children and young people need to be reassured that it's OK to not feel OK, especially when someone (or something) they love has died, or is no longer as present in their lives for some reason. It's also important to reassure them that people grieve in different ways – there are no rules and no predictable patterns to grief. You can feel deeply upset one day, but not the next. And then you can feel upset again the day after. Grief can come in waves like this, and it can last for a long time too. And it's important to reassure children and young people that it's *also* OK to feel OK. I've spoken with quite a few children and young people who felt guilty for *not* feeling upset all the time, as if that was what they were supposed to feel.

The Bible tells us that Jesus wept when his friend Lazarus died. It's likely Jesus already knew that he would soon bring Lazarus back to life again, but when he saw Lazarus's sister Mary weeping, John writes, Jesus was deeply moved and he wept too.[14] He mourned with those who were mourning.[15] It is deeply reassuring to know that we worship a God who understands our pain and suffering, and the spaces we host for prayer should reflect this.

'It's nice to know that I can go somewhere to talk about my friend's death,' wrote a teenage boy after visiting a prayer space in his school. I hope that there were other people he felt he could share his joy and his suffering with, and other places where he felt he could go to do this, but if there weren't, I'm glad that he felt like he could trust the prayer space, and the people in it, to be a safe space.

Reflect and Pray

1. Imagine that you are doing the Character Cards activity with a friend or a family member. Think of two or three things about them – characteristics – that you see in them and like. And now, if you're feeling brave, message them and tell them about the exercise and what you've been thinking about them.

2. Dr VanderWeele says, 'One way to get more comfortable with forgiveness is to practise small acts in everyday life.'[16] Is there someone you need to forgive,

even if what they've said or done is something small? Talk with God about this now. If it helps, find a stone or some other solid object and do the Forgiveness Stones activity for yourself.

3. Do you know a child or a young person who has lost someone they loved, or perhaps they've lost a pet? Pray that God would comfort them as they mourn.

PRAYER ACTIVITY: THE EMPTY CHAIR

What is it?

When someone we love leaves us or dies, they leave a gap – an 'empty chair' – in our lives. We miss them.

This activity offers a simple, safe place for pupils to consider and express a bit of how they feel about someone they have loved and lost. It encourages pupils to reflect on the good memories, but it also allows for, and affirms, the sad ones too. It's OK to not be OK.

How does it work?

For this activity, the main thing that you need is a nice wooden chair (preferably not a regular school chair). Then you'll need some luggage tags and pens, or paper and pegs, or sticky notes, and some cushions too. It's handy to also have a box of tissues.

Put the chair in a corner of the room, away from other activities that are likely to be busy or noisy. Surround the chair with cushions. If you want to, you can make the chair look extra-special with some fabric or spotlights. Then put the luggage tags and pens beside the chair. There is also a poem that you might like to print out and laminate (see below).

Who is it for?

This activity was created with secondary school pupils (teenagers) in mind. However, with careful hosting, it could also be adapted for primary school children.

Any other information?

We would recommend that you discuss this activity with the pastoral staff in the school before including it in your prayer space. It works best if there is an adult alongside who can listen if pupils want to talk.

Instructions

When someone we love leaves or dies, we miss them. It's like they leave an empty chair at the table of our lives. Is there someone you miss?

If you want to, you can write the name of the person, and something that you remember about them, onto one of the labels and attach it to the chair. Say a quiet thank you for the good memories that you have of them. If you want to, you can talk with God about your feelings too. Take your time. It might be helpful to talk to an adult afterwards as well.

A little story . . .

When Matt Rushby, a local youth worker, noticed that pupils often used the prayer spaces that his team were hosting in local schools to process experiences of loss and feelings of grief, he decided to try and create a new prayer activity that would help them.

Matt had recently lost his own grandfather, and now, when the whole family gathered for mealtimes and celebrations, the chair that his grandfather used to sit in was noticeably vacant. The space that his grandfather had occupied in their home, and in their hearts, was now empty. Drawing on his own suffering, Matt created The Empty Chair activity and wrote a poem to go with it, and these have since been used in hundreds of prayer spaces.

The Empty Chair

I look for you, but you're not there.
Instead, there's just an Empty Chair.
As people laugh – you would have too,
But you're not here, and I miss you.
I think of favourite memories,
Of times we spent, just you and me;
Your face, your smile, your favourite stuff.
At times like these it's really tough.
I'm thankful for the fun we had,
But right now . . . I'm just feeling sad.
So, I'll turn my sadness into prayer,
As I look at your Empty Chair.

–Matt Rushby

Please help us with the world. I want to fix it.

7

Acting Justly, Loving Mercy, Walking Humbly[1]

Being reconciled with the world

What pupils say: *'Thank you for this prayer space. It has made me feel better about my life.'*—Boy, aged eight

What teachers say: *'I've seen a different side to the pupils this afternoon; I never thought they would engage with something like this, and I didn't know they had so many big issues going on in their lives.'*—Teacher, UK

* * *

Prayer spaces can help children and young people become reconciled with the world in a culture where 'the world' is constantly fed to them via their digital devices, mediated and manipulated in all sorts of opaque ways. In a matter of clicks they can be exposed to wonder and devastation in the natural world, to incredible innovation and terrible suffering in the human world, and to the inequalities and injustices that exist everywhere.

Almost every day, children and young people receive a flood of information (and misinformation) about violence and war, poverty and all kinds of suffering, often broadcast live on social media by people who are wherever the action is. They can become quickly engaged and enraged by injustice, but they can also feel overwhelmed with anxiety about the desperate state of the planet. Mental health author Lily-Jo writes, 'It may sound absurd to say that a huge proportion of our young people are experiencing anxiety as a result of worrying about the end of the world, but the results of various studies support that assertion.'[2]

In Eugene Peterson's paraphrased version of Paul's letter to the Colossian church, he writes that '[in Christ] all the broken and dislocated pieces of the universe – people and things, animals and atoms – get properly fixed and fit together in vibrant harmonies'.[3] It all belongs because of God's great love for the world. In this chapter I'm going to focus on three ways that prayer spaces can help children and people to love the world too:

- Praying for the world
- Engaging with injustice
- Experiencing creation

(In the third section, you'll also find some practical tips on how to run outdoor prayer spaces.)

Praying for the World

There are lots of prayer activities that enable children and young people to pray for the world. You've probably seen some, and you may have even created a few yourself too, but here is a selection of my favourites:

- Pupils choose a national flag from a list/website and colour in a flag shape accordingly. They write or draw a thought or a prayer for that nation on the back, and then pin their flags onto the wall.
- Pupils write or draw their thoughts or prayers for different nations onto some white footballs ('soccer balls', for my American friends). This activity works particularly well during sports competitions.
- Spread a large world map on the floor. Pupils place battery-powered candles or small stones/glass beads onto particular nations to represent their thoughts or prayers.
- Hang some inflatable globes from the ceiling. Pupils write or draw their thoughts or prayers onto small sticky notes and stick them onto specific nations/regions.
- Attach a large world map onto a wall and surround it with printouts of current news headlines. Pupils write

or draw their thoughts or prayers onto small sticky notes and stick them onto the map or onto the news headlines.

I've used activities like these, in both primary and secondary school prayer spaces, to help children and young people reflect on, and pray for, the world, and two significant things have caught my attention. The first is how multicultural schools often are, and therefore how connected pupils already feel to many nations. They truly are global citizens in ways that my generation simply doesn't understand. When I went to school on the edge of east London, every single pupil spoke English as their first language. Twenty years later, the primary school in north London that my middle daughter went to had pupils with fifty-two different first languages (including sign language), which probably meant that there were more than fifty-two nationalities represented. Many of the pupils we meet in prayer spaces have friends and family around the world, and so when they use activities like Pray for the World, they are often thinking of and praying for people they know and love.

The second thing that has caught my attention is the worry and anxiety that children and young people feel about what is going on in the world, in addition to the things that are going on at school or at home. Here are some examples of things that pupils pinned to a Worry Wall in their prayer space:

- *'I am worried about those in Venezuela who are in crisis.'*
- *'I am worried about XXX becoming prime minister.'*
- *'I am worried about how the Earth is being polluted.'*
- *'I am worried about Climate Change and the environment. Why don't you save it?'*
- *'I am worried about terrorists.' (It's worth mentioning that the child who wrote this also added, 'and small portions of lunch', which just goes to illustrate the range and scale of things that children worry about!)*
- *'When I was little there was a war in my country and we came to England to be safe, but most of my family couldn't come and I'm worried for them.'*

In another prayer space, I noticed that a teacher looked tearful, so I went across to talk with her. She showed me a couple of poignant sticky notes at their Pray for the World activity, and then nodded towards a girl on the other side of the room. 'She wrote those,' she said. 'I just told her off for not doing her homework. I had no idea what she was going through.'

The last worry on the list above is unusual because it was born out of lived experience. Most children's and young people's worries aren't born out of experience, but out of the information (and misinformation) they receive about conflict and war, natural disasters, environmental crises, political turmoil and so on; things that they see and read on their digital devices. The relentlessness of these reports and real-time videos can be overwhelming, leaving children and young people feeling both numb and anxious.

Give Your Worries

Prayer spaces can be a healthy response to this numbness and to feelings of worry and anxiety about the world, because they offer children and young people simple, creative ways to express how they feel, with or without words. Placing a stone on a map doesn't require words, for example, but it is a way of saying, 'I feel something.' Writing the name of a nation on a heart-shaped sticky note can be a way of acknowledging, 'I am carrying this nation deep within my heart.' Placing that sticky note on a larger heart shape that represents God's heart can be a powerful act of intercession.

Some prayer activities also offer pupils practical ways to engage further, giving them something to actually do beyond the prayer space itself. Praying is doing something, of course, but some of the activities also suggest further action that children and young people can take if they want to (see the 'Engaging with Injustice' section below for some examples). And finally, for many children and young people, prayer spaces introduce them to the God who hears their worries and cares for them. 'Give all your worries and cares to God,' writes the apostle Peter, 'for he cares about you.'[4] And not only does God care about them, but God cares about the things that they care about too.

Engaging with Injustice

Ian's local primary school asked if his team could run a prayer space for them, and they decided to try out some new prayer activities, including one called Refugee Rucksacks. In an email, Ian explained:

> We had a rucksack and a pile of random items, some useful and some personal. The pupils were invited to imagine that they were refugees and that they'd been given just five minutes to flee from their homes. 'Which of these items would you take with you?' we asked. They engaged with the task as we expected, some choosing to take the PlayStation or some DVDs, but leave the water, the rice and the First Aid kit. But then they started to take things a bit more seriously. They

wondered where they might be going, how difficult things might get, and how they might not have access to food or water for days on end . . . the initially chosen items were soon replaced! But then a little girl put up her hand. She was cuddling a teddy bear, which was nearly the same size as she was, and she said, 'I feel like a refugee.' When I asked why, she said, 'Because my parents are getting divorced and I don't know which country I will be living in.' From the back of the room, her teacher mouthed to me, 'I'll chat to her parents later in the week.'

Lifeboat Prayers

For two months in the middle of 2015, desperate people tried to flee the civil war in northern Syria by squeezing onto makeshift boats to escape across the Mediterranean Sea and into Europe. Many of these boats didn't arrive at their destination. And then, for a moment in September 2015, TV screens and social media feeds around the world featured one harrowing image – the lifeless body of two-year-old Alan Kurdi, a Syrian boy of Kurdish-ethnic background, washed up on a beach. When Simon, a local youth worker, saw the news reports, he wept. 'I've got a young child too,' he thought. 'What can I do?'

Simon and another youth minister had been invited to run a prayer space (they called it Soul Space) at their local high school, and they wanted to include something about social justice, something, as Simon put it, that 'wasn't just about "me". We wanted to encourage the pupils to pray, but then to do something about what they'd prayed. We wanted the pupils to understand that prayer doesn't have to be passive, and that we can sometimes take action and become part of God's way of answering our prayers.'

Having been moved by what they'd seen on their screens, and having found some useful information online, they decided to find the largest inflatable boat that they could fit into the drama studio and use it to create a new prayer activity, which they called Lifeboat Prayers. The instructions for the activity went something like this:

> A refugee is someone who has had to leave their home because of danger. People do desperate things when their lives are in unimaginable danger. They take huge risks to get to safety, such as travelling in unsafe, overcrowded boats, and they can take very little with them.
>
> Look at the items in the boat. The pillow represents our warm, comfortable homes. The water represents the food and drink we need each day. The photograph represents family and friends. The pens and paper represent education.

> If you want to, you can write a hope or a prayer for those people who have had to leave their homes and who have lost precious possessions.

Throughout the week, pupils climbed into the inflatable boat and wrote their hopes and prayers for the refugees onto small brown luggage tags, which they tied onto the oarlocks along the sides of the boat. The staff were amazed at how these teenagers engaged with the activity, and one even commented, 'This is like spiritual oxygen for these young people.'

Towards the end of the week, the head teacher invited the local Member of Parliament (MP) to visit their Soul Space. When the MP saw what the pupils had been doing and read the luggage tags, he was deeply moved. Having received permission from the school, he wrote a letter to the British prime minister and enclosed some of the luggage tags, describing them as 'a petition' for change. And so some of the pupils' prayers reached Number 10 Downing Street, the seat of power in the United Kingdom – while of course they also reached heaven, the place of ultimate power in the universe.

Making A Difference

I've seen prayer activities themed around all sorts of (in)justice issues, including food poverty, water pollution, species extinction and various other effects of Climate Change, people trafficking, racism, lack of educational opportunities for girls in some parts of the world, and so on. For example, teenagers at a Fast Fashion prayer activity sewed buttons onto a T-shirt as they read about poor working conditions for very young children in factories in India, and then silently offered their hopes, wishes and prayers.

Children and young people seem to be wired to recognise unfairness and injustice, and they instinctively want to do something about these issues, but they often don't know what to do, or they feel overwhelmed and hopeless because the issues seem too big. According to author Lily-Jo:

> The glut of information they consume can lead to exacerbated feelings of hopelessness, and that hopelessness is due to a psychological effect called 'pseudo-inefficiency', which is when a person realises the problem they are faced with has such a large scope, their small contribution to change feels meaningless, so they don't know what to do and may end up doing nothing. It doesn't help that the media focuses on sensationalism and scandal, rather than presenting solutions. Consequently, young people are paralysed between the fear that if they do not do something to save the world they are doomed, and

> the hopelessness that nothing they do will have a significant impact.[5]

Added to this, children and young people are often confused and frustrated that the Church doesn't seem to respond to issues of injustice in the ways that they think it could and, perhaps, should. When we explored this theme during one of our conferences, Jo Herbert-James (who was working with the Tearfund charity at the time) pointed out that for many teenagers in church, engaging with injustice was central to their Christian faith and essential to the way they followed Jesus. 'If you haven't developed your theology of justice,' she said to the conference participants, many of whom were church leaders, 'and if you aren't practically engaging with issues of injustice, then you won't reach, nor keep, young people.'

In the Barna Group's 2023 study of 25,000 Christian teenagers across twenty-six nations, 37 per cent said that the Church should be 'encouraging people to address injustice and advocate for meaningful change'.[6] In his reflections at the end of the survey summary, UK Christian leader Krish Kandiah commented:

> I have personally witnessed the passion and enthusiasm of teenagers to pursue justice . . . I believe

> young people have huge potential to make a positive difference in the world, but [this] survey shows us that many young people have lost confidence that change is possible . . . I think some churches have reduced teenagers to consumers. We provide programmes for children and young people to attend rather than opportunities for them to use their creativity, vision, skills, talents and leadership to make a difference.[7]

Like Kandiah, I believe that children and young people have huge potential to pursue justice and make a positive difference in the world. The answer isn't to hide them away from the grim reality of injustice and suffering in the world, but to offer them honest, practical and hopeful ways to respond, and I believe that prayer spaces can do just that.

One of the first prayer spaces I was involved with took place just before Christmas that year. We wanted to include a justice-themed prayer activity, so we asked the staff if the school already had any charity connections, and they mentioned Crisis, the UK national charity for people experiencing homelessness. As part of its Christmas appeal that winter, Crisis was asking people to donate socks, so we decided to create a prayer activity around this theme. Guess what we called it. Yep, Crisis Socks!

We pinned photos of homeless young people onto the walls alongside some information and statistics taken directly from the Crisis website. Then we cut out dozens of paper sock-shapes, onto which we invited pupils to write or draw their hopes or prayers for those who were homeless. One of the first pupils to do the activity was a seventeen-year-old girl, and she seemed quite distressed as she looked at the photos and read what we'd pinned to the walls. She returned the following lunchtime to write on another sock-shape, and then again the lunchtime after that. When she came back for her fifth visit on the Friday she asked, 'What more can I do? I need to do something about this.'

When I'm teaching about prayer, I often throw in a warning about prayer being dangerous. It's dangerous for lots of reasons, but mainly because sometimes when we pray, God's reply is a simple, 'Go on then!' In these moments, we might not hear God's audible voice, but we definitely feel something urgent, compelling us into action.

'No, God, you don't understand. I was asking you to send *other* people. You know, more workers for the harvest fields and all that – people with skills and *abilities*.'

'But I'm not particularly bothered about *ability*,' replies God warmly. 'I'm more interested in *availability*, for open hearts and a bit of compassion. And wow, when you prayed just now, I really felt it – your heart was wide open, full of compassion. So I've decided to send you. But don't worry, I'll go with you.' We pray our prayers, and sometimes God answers our prayers by sending us. That's what the 24–7 Prayer movement has always been about – prayer that becomes mission and justice – because, in our experience, these things are inseparable.

'That's fantastic!' I said to the Crisis Socks girl. We talked some more about what she'd like to do and then we put her in touch with the local Salvation Army group who were running outreach and support programmes for homeless people in the town, so she went and joined in with what they were doing. And another prayer began to be answered.

Experiencing Creation

During the Covid-19 pandemic, lots of schools were unable or unwilling to allow visitors in to host prayer spaces in schools. Figuring out how to run a socially distanced prayer space where no one could touch anything that anyone else had touched (without it first being wiped clean) wasn't easy. A few brave churches and schools managed to come up with ways to do it, but most simply waited for the pandemic to pass. And then some people spotted a potential solution – take the prayer space outside. We'd tracked and supported a few outdoor prayer spaces over the years, but all of a sudden everyone was doing it.

'The outdoors is the original natural prayer space,' said Jane Gillis when we asked about her prayer spaces in and around Bristol. 'Why wouldn't you want to host a prayer space outside? There are just so many things that tap into your senses, and you can use all of them to help children and young people connect with God.' Jane has been working with children and young people in all sorts of educational and church settings for twenty-five years, often with a focus on 'the big outdoors'. She even told us that she'd previously led some Stone Age workshops, but despite being very curious about this, we managed to keep our conversation focused on prayer spaces! 'We've all experienced the presence of God in nature at some point in our lives,' Jane continued. 'In fact, most of us have done so this week, maybe without even realising it.'

Just think about that statement for a moment. Think about when you've been outside this week. What did you see – what caught your attention? Maybe it was that moment when you marvelled at a rainbow stretching across the sky after a rainstorm. Or when you crouched down to examine the intricate beauty of a spider's web heavy with morning dew. Or when you stepped out of your back door and stared at the stars or the planets in the night sky. Maybe you even whispered, 'Wow!' in one of these moments? Whether you realised it or not, something in that spontaneous expression of awe and wonder was your spirit reaching out to the God who mastercrafted it all.

I'm not suggesting that we only, or even mostly, experience the presence of God in nature. Personality types probably play a part in where and how we each connect with God. And besides, it could be argued that God is actually more present in the person behind you in the supermarket queue, and even in those noisy next-door neighbours, than in anything else that God has created in the entire universe. Volcanoes and angelfish and giant redwood trees are the product of the imagination of God, but people (even the annoying ones) are made in the *image* of God.

Having said all that, plenty of people who believe in God say that they feel closer to God when they've escaped the crowds, and when they're surrounded by nature in some way . . . hiking on a mountain, walking along a beach, exploring a forest, watching a sunrise or a sunset. And even those who say they don't believe in God often say something similar, but without the 'God' bit. They describe it as 'connecting spiritually' or 'feeling most alive' instead. My hunch is that we're all talking about the same thing.

'Nature is a ready-made prayer space,' Jane said, warming to her theme. 'It's already beautiful, so we don't need to spend too much time making our outdoor prayer spaces look great. And there's all sorts of natural stuff that we can use for our prayer activities too: sticks and stones and trees and clouds and the weather and creepy-crawlies and so on.' Jane described a few of the activities she's created for use outdoors, all of which seem to have intriguing titles: Binocular Boggle, Challenge Swamp, Forest Listening, to name a few.

Muddy Mess is a sorry-themed prayer activity, and you can probably guess what it involves. The pupils begin by reading the information sheet, or listening while one of the volunteers reads it to them: 'We all get into a mess sometimes, especially when we do things that are selfish or wrong. Have you done anything selfish or wrong recently?' After the pupils have had a few moments to think, they are invited to plunge their hands into a bucket of mud. 'What can we do to sort out this mess?' the information card continues. 'Saying sorry is a good way to start sorting out the mess in our lives, and when we say sorry to someone, it's an opportunity for them to forgive us too. The Bible says that God always forgives us – God always makes us clean again. When you're ready, wash your hands in the bowl of water next to the bucket. If you want to, you can whisper a sorry prayer to God while you're doing this.' Of all the sorry-themed prayer activities in our online library, I think this is my favourite.

'We've also created a simple prayer activity called Clouds,' Jane said, 'which invites pupils to lie on a mat and just look up at the clouds. (Obviously you can only really do this on a day when there are clouds!) I think there's something really healthy about looking at the expanse of sky above us and reflecting on how small we are in comparison. I remember having a lovely conversation with a young girl about this. As she lay on the mat staring at the clouds, I asked her what she felt God might want to say to her. She thought for a few moments, still gazing up into the sky, and then said, "I think God is holding me – God has got me. I think God is saying, 'I'm big and you're small, but it's all right because I've got you.'" I was amazed! I actually think that children find it a lot easier to connect with God in nature than we do. It's why I love trying to see the world through their eyes. It really is wonderful.'

Rach and her team of volunteers helped to organise an outdoor prayer space at a primary school in

Farnham. They were offered a small hut behind the school to set up some of the prayer activities, so it wasn't as 'al fresco' as Jane's, but they made good use of the outdoor space, and they decided to do all of the end-of-session feedback beneath a large tree, because there was more room there for everyone to sit down. After one of the sessions, Rach asked the usual questions: 'How did you feel about the activities?' 'What did you like?' 'What was your favourite?' One of the little boys stuck his hand up and said, 'I said thank you for my mum.' It was a lovely thing for him to say, but Rach didn't understand why the teachers sitting around the edges of the class were in tears. It wasn't until the end of the day that one of them told her that this little boy had never spoken out loud in school before.

When we asked Jane for some tips on how to run great prayer spaces outdoors, this was her advice:

1. Use the natural stuff outside for your prayer activities. Use physical objects like trees and stones and leaves. Use the weather – sunlight, clouds, wind, etc. And definitely use the seasons. It's possible to include a few prayer activities outside that you would usually use in an indoor classroom, but it's better to make the most of God's natural resources.

2. If possible, use an area of the school site that isn't too noisy, where the pupils won't get interrupted or distracted.
3. Unless the weather is incredibly bad (e.g. gale-force winds or torrential rain), you can probably still do your prayer space. Just make sure that the pupils (and your team) are dressed appropriately. Ask the school to contact parents/carers about this.
4. Following on from that, make sure that quite a few of your activities are still OK to use even if it rains a bit. Use waterproof tents and other weatherproof resources.
5. And in case it gets too bad, have an escape plan. Work out where you will shelter, and where you can relocate your prayer space to, if the weather gets crazy.
6. Think carefully about security if your prayer space is taking place over a couple of days. You might need to pack up at the end of the first day and set up again the following morning, which isn't ideal, but it may be the safest option.
7. Ideally, invite small groups (of twelve to fifteen pupils) to use the prayer space rather than whole classes. This will help to keep the noise down and to ensure that the pupils slow down.
8. If possible, and especially if you are running your outdoor prayer space in a primary school, invite the

parents/carers to visit the space at the end of one of the school days, preferably after a few of the classes have participated so the parents can see what the children have been doing.

9. Before you run a full-day outdoor prayer space, you might want to start by 'test driving' your prayer activities with some children and young people whom you know. This way you can practise guiding them around the prayer space and see how well the prayer activities work, especially if they're new ones.
10. Keep it simple. Trust me, it'll work better than you think.

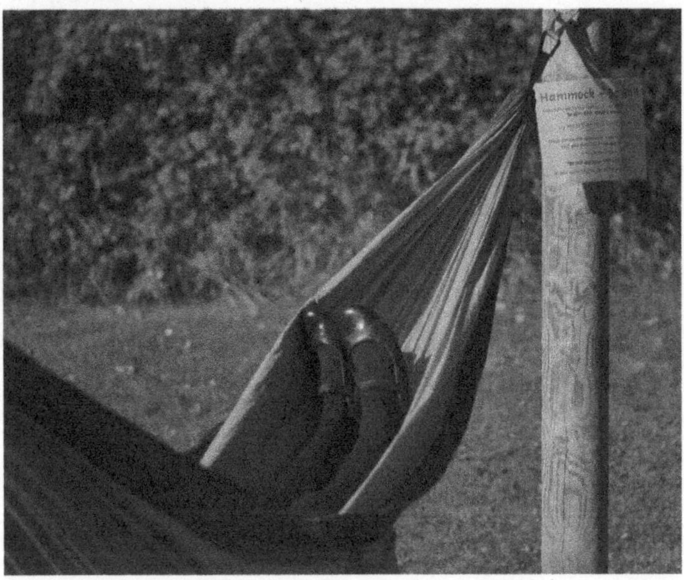

Reflect and Pray

1. Open whatever map app you've got on your phone, or find an actual world map or a globe. Who do you know who lives or works in another country? Find that country on your map. Now ask God to give you a Bible verse or something else that you can encourage them with, and then send it on to them.

2. What (in)justice issue makes you the most sad or angry? Take a few moments to pray about it. Ask God to show you how you can become an answer to your own prayers, even in some small way.

3. Make some time over the coming week to go for a slow walk. It could be along a sandy beach or beside a river. It could be through a forest or up a hill. Before you set out, switch your phone off. Ask God to be with you as you walk . . . and just listen.

PRAYER ACTIVITY: CARDBOARD HOME

Cardboard Home is a popular prayer activity, and you'll find it being used in prayer spaces in lots of places - maybe because it's very easy for children to understand. Or maybe because it's so visceral, and it engages the whole body in prayer. Or maybe, sadly, because homelessness is a justice issue everywhere. It's not just a developing nation's justice issue. It's a justice issue in my neighbourhood, and in your neighbourhood too.

What is it?

Although it's hard to find accurate statistics, it is estimated that up to 100 million children may be living on the streets around the world.[8]

There are many people throughout the world who are not as fortunate as we are, people who do not have homes, who are not in touch with their families and who do not even have a regular supply of food and water. This activity encourages pupils to think about street children who are of a similar age to them and to think about how it would feel if they themselves did not have a home to live in, but just a cardboard box.

How does it work?

You can do this activity with just a few large cardboard boxes (large enough for your pupils to crawl inside) and some pens, but it will help to have some laminated images of homeless people, including street children, as well. You could surround the boxes with some 'clean' rubbish to add to the feeling of being on the street.

Put the cardboard box on its side in a corner of your prayer space, and place the images inside and in front of the box, along with the pens. Invite the pupils to crawl inside the cardboard box and look at the photos.

Who is it for?

This activity works best with younger children, but I have used it in secondary schools too.

Any other information?

This activity works best when one of the prayer space hosts is alongside the box, asking questions like: How do you think street children feel? What might their hopes and fears be? The host can then encourage the pupils to write or draw their thoughts or prayers onto the box.

Instructions

Most of us have nice warm, clean homes. Sadly, millions of children around the world don't. Some children have no homes or are forced to move about from place to place. Sit in the box. How would it feel to live in a box like this? If you want to, you can write or draw your thoughts or prayers on the box.

A little story . . .

Young children at a homelessness-themed prayer activity in a primary school crawled into the large cardboard boxes and then looked at photos of other children their age who were living in cardboard boxes on street corners. Here's a selection of the things they wrote (unedited for spelling):

- *'Sad 😢'*
- *'Lonely 😢'*
- *'it's a squeez'*
- *'get me a pilow or a dovey'*
- *'Dear God, hellp the boy in the box. Armen'*
- *'Dear God, I gust want to tell you People in difrient countries dont have beds and I want you to give them a bed so they can lie down properly'*

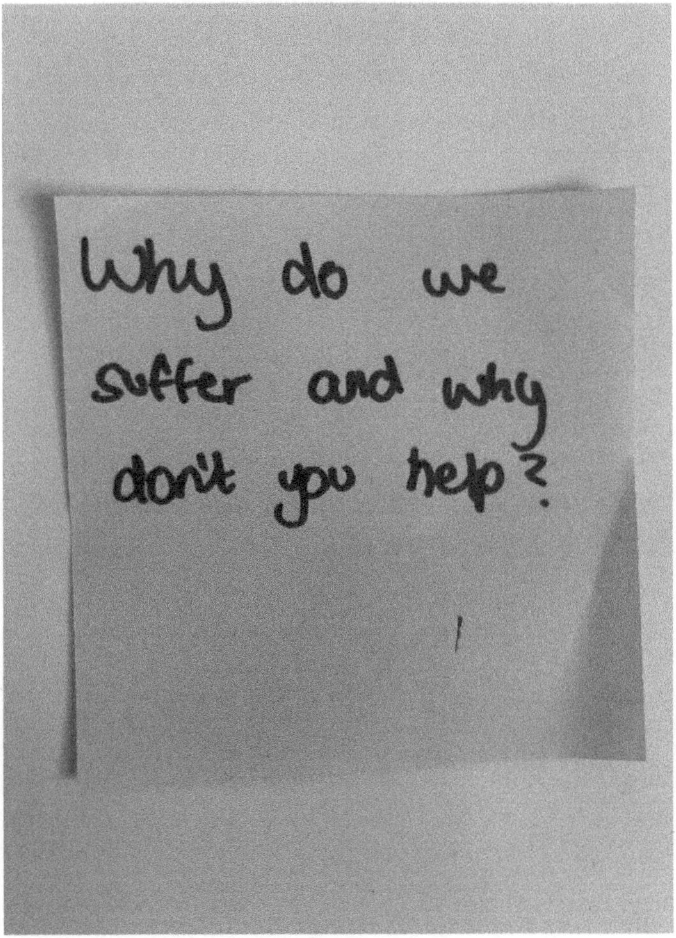
Why do we suffer and why don't you help?

8

Seeking and Finding[1]

Being reconciled with God

What pupils say: *'I've enjoyed it even though I'm not a Christian. It really helps you believe/find/communicate with God.'*—Boy, aged fourteen

What teachers say: *'This week has helped me appreciate my role, my very unique role, much more. The week also helped my personal spiritual journey and I found myself being drawn closer to God.'*—Head of RE, UK

* * *

In the last of these four chapters about reconciliation, I want to focus on how prayer spaces can help children and young people become reconciled with their spirituality: how they can become more aware of, and connected with, their spiritual lives – and ultimately with God – in a culture that seems to be increasingly secularised.

In the UK, and in some other nations too, there is evidence of increasing numbers of children and young people joining particular churches and church networks, but the overall picture is mixed. For example, in 2020, the Church of England reported that 38 per cent of their churches had no 0–16s whatsoever, and that Sunday attendance among that age group in the UK had dropped below 100,000 for the first time on record.[2] On the other side of the Atlantic, at first glance the statistics look a bit better. Research conducted by Barna in 2023 found that '65% of US teens identify as Christian',[3] but when they scratched below the surface they discovered that only half of these teens equated 'being a Christian' with any kind of 'commitment to follow Jesus'. And this figure dropped even further, to 17 per cent, once these teens reached the eighteen to twenty-two age range. Barna described this as 'a sharp decline'.

As we heard in the previous chapter, one of the reasons for this decline may be that children and young people don't feel the Church is relevant any more because it isn't making a difference on the issues that matter to them, such as poverty, equality and injustice.[4] Or maybe they struggle to believe the Church's 'God is love' message when that God doesn't seem to be making much of a difference in a suffering world. However, we mustn't mistake a lack of interest in the institution of the Church – nor even an ambivalence about God's nature – for a lack of spiritual hunger and thirst. It might simply be that we haven't fully recognised yet what it is that children and young people are really hungry and thirsty for.

The prayer activities in our online library invite children and young people to 'taste and see that the Lord is good'[5] for themselves, rather than trying to force-feed them anything. The instructions almost always include the phrase 'if you want to . . .', and we really mean it. Using prayer activities should always be optional. The remarkable thing is that children and young people really do seem to want to pray; they want to talk with God – even those who initially say that they don't even believe in God. While there are all sorts of aspects to this that we could explore, the three areas I'm going to focus on are:

- Anger and suffering
- Asking big questions
- Encountering God (aka miracles?)

Anger and Suffering

'What should we do with this prayer?' asked one of the volunteers, pointing at something a pupil had written at one of the prayer activities. 'Should we remove it?' For a moment I was confused – why would you remove a prayer? – but then I saw what she was pointing at.

Possibly the most raw and honest prayer that I've ever seen in a prayer space, and it was only two words: 'f*** cancer' (the prayer on the big sheet of paper in front of me included the letters I've replaced here with asterisks).

I was visiting a secondary school prayer space in my town. Ben was leading the team and he told me that a class of thirteen- to fourteen-year-olds had just left the room. 'It felt a bit tense right from the start,' he explained, 'like there was some kind of atmosphere. When we introduced the session and began to explain the bit about what Christians believe about prayer, the pupils were very quiet and they seemed a bit uncomfortable. It wasn't until halfway through the lesson that we found out why – a close relative of one of the boys had recently died of cancer. The other pupils, and the teacher, were aware of this, and I think they were a bit unsure about how the boy was going to handle the prayer space. He did get a bit emotional during the session, but the other pupils were actually very respectful and supportive, sombre even. And then the boy wrote the prayer with a swear word at the Letting Go prayer activity in the corner.'

Sometimes it's important to curate your prayer activities, especially ones that invite pupils to write something on sticky notes or on something else that will remain visible for the duration of the prayer space. On one occasion, I remember a pupil writing 'thank God for cheese' on a sticky note and within just a few hours it had multiplied and there were dozens of other 'thank God for cheese' notes. A similar thing happened when a pupil posted 'pray for penguins'! Although I am definitely grateful for cheese, and I'm also concerned about the plight of penguins and other endangered animals around the world, it's still OK to remove 95 per cent of the sticky notes when they multiply like this.

But was it OK to remove the boy's prayer? If someone had graffitied the swear word on a wall somewhere else in the school, it would have been quickly removed or painted over, and if the pupil had been caught, they would've been in a lot of trouble, which is probably why the volunteer asked the question, 'What should we do with this prayer? Should we remove it?'

A few years later, I was invited to speak at the Anglican Schools Conference in Brisbane, Australia. The conference centre's auditorium was much bigger than I'd imagined it would be, and it was filled with head teachers, RE coordinators and school chaplains from all over Australia. I suddenly felt very intimidated, and I regretted not bringing a smarter shirt. The first speaker was amazing – she was the youngest female commander in the Australian army and she told some extraordinary stories of courage and faith – and then it was my turn. Standing at the centre of the enormous, empty stage, I took a deep breath and launched into my tightly planned talk, which was filled with stories about prayer spaces in schools and illustrated with slides that scrolled on the giant screen behind me. And then, about halfway through, a terrifying thing happened . . . I heard myself start to tell an unscripted story that began with a volunteer asking, 'What should we do with this prayer?' Outwardly, I continued to tell the story, while inwardly, all I could think was, *I'm about to tell a story about a prayer that includes a swear word to a roomful of head teachers!*

'Should we remove it?' I asked the packed auditorium, repeating the volunteer's second question. 'I don't think so,' I continued. 'Imagine if that boy had returned to the prayer space later in the day and found that his prayer had been removed – how would he feel? What would that say to him? That God wasn't interested in his pain? That God didn't care about his rage? That God only listens when we're polite, when we say and pray nice words? That his prayers were wholly unacceptable?'

It won't come as a surprise to many of you who do public speaking when I say that after doing my talk, I felt very vulnerable and insecure. I almost always feel this way, even if the talk has gone well. And on this occasion, I was also genuinely worried that I'd offended some people, and that I'd wasted an opportunity to inspire these leaders to get started with prayer spaces in Australian schools.

However, as soon as the host announced the coffee break, a woman rushed down the auditorium steps towards me and, to my surprise, gave me a huge hug! 'Thank you for swearing!' she said with a tearful smile. (There are two things that I'd like to say at this point. First, I didn't actually swear when I told the story. And second, you'll be pleased to know that this was the first and last time I received this particular feedback after doing any public speaking!) When she got her breath back, the woman told me her story. She was a vicar, probably in her early fifties, and her son had died of cancer the previous year. When this happened, she found prayer really difficult. She felt like a hypocrite, leading prayers for her congregation every Sunday, but unable to talk with God personally herself – silenced by the pain and the rage inside her.

After six months like this, she couldn't bear it any longer, so she went out for a long walk in the fields near where she lived, determined to pray. But when she opened her mouth to speak, she was shocked by what spilled out. Instead of well-constructed sentences there came groans and cries, lots of shouting and, to her horror, even a little bit of swearing. And when it was all over, she felt desperately guilty about hurling profanities – words that she would never normally use – at God in prayer, and the shame of having done so silenced her once again. Since that day, she hadn't prayed personally.

'Until this morning, that is,' she said, with more tears and an even bigger smile. 'When you told that story, I heard God whisper to me that's how he feels about cancer too. It's OK for me to not be OK – God is OK with that.'

We know all this, in theory at least. Of course God is OK with us not being OK, and lots of the prayer-songs in the book of Psalms affirm this. As far as I'm aware, there are no profanities in the original languages, but the psalms are nonetheless filled with pain and rage and unfiltered emotion. If we had the space, I'd include the whole of Psalm 88 at this point. (If you've got the time, and a Bible handy, I'd recommend putting this little book down for a few minutes to read Psalm 88 for yourself. Try the NIVUK translation first. Read it slowly, and then read the same psalm in Eugene Peterson's paraphrased book, *The Message*. You won't regret it.)

One of the remarkable things about Psalm 88 is that it's all desolation, from start to finish – there's no consolation at the end, no comfort. There's no quick fix, no easy solution to the psalmist's pain and anger. I've often wondered if a worship leader will ever be brave enough to announce one Sunday that they've written a new song for the congregation to sing, and that it's based on Psalm 88. 'Come on everyone, join in . . . "I am overwhelmed with troubles, and my life draws near to death . . . I am confined and cannot escape; my eyes are dim with grief."' But this prayer-song is in the Bible for a reason. And at the very least, it should invite us to give voice to our own pain and rage.

Children and young people (and even some not-so-young people) can feel silenced by the pain and rage inside them. Some of them feel this way because, like the vicar in Australia, they feel that if they opened their mouths to say something, the words that would spill out would not be OK, and so they say nothing. Others feel silenced because they simply can't find *any* words to express how they feel – words just don't seem to be enough.

Prayer Without Words

When I'm delivering the short introduction at the start of a prayer space session, there's an illustration I sometimes use to make this point. I ask the pupils to imagine that I've just received a telephone call to say that my wife and three daughters have been seriously hurt in a car accident, and that they may not survive. Then I tell them that I'm going to pray two prayers, and that I'm going to ask them afterwards which prayer felt most real. For the first prayer I close my eyes, bow my head and put my hands together and pray something like this, 'Dear God, be with my wife and daughters. I'm really worried. Please save them. Amen.' And then, for the second prayer, I clench my fists, curl into a ball, and scream! (I aim for something loud enough to shock the class in the room, but not to panic the class next door.) When the nervous laughter dies down, I ask which they think felt like a *real* prayer, which felt the most *authentic.* It's fascinating how many pupils still choose the first prayer, because 'it had words', because 'you said Dear God and Amen', because 'how can a scream be a prayer?'.

Or if I want to use a slightly less dramatic illustration, I hold up a sticky note with some scribbling on it and I ask the class, 'How many of you think that this could be a prayer?' At first, usually no one puts their hand up, so I ask another question. 'How many of you think that this definitely couldn't be a prayer?' Most of the class put their hands up, but a few hands always stay down. 'Hang on,' I say, 'some of you didn't put your hands up then. Let me ask one more time then: how many of you think that this *could* be a prayer?' This time, a few hands will go up, and when I ask them why, they say things like, 'Maybe the person is angry?' or 'Maybe the person is confused?' And bingo, we've just stumbled into one of the great mysteries about prayer. Prayer doesn't require words.

Perhaps a couple of the greatest gifts that prayer spaces offer to children and young people are, first, the opportunity and the permission to express some of their pain and rage in simple, creative ways, with or without words; and then, second, the affirmation that we can address and express these feelings to God – that doing so *is* prayer – and that God hears and receives it all. God doesn't flinch or recoil from how we express ourselves.

God isn't even offended by our accusations. God isn't a schoolteacher who returns our prayers like homework with 'Could do better' or 'Rephrase this please' scribbled across the top. God simply receives all the pain and rage and responds with, 'It's OK, I'm here, I love you.'

'Moments like these,' writes Pete Greig, 'remind me that comfort can sometimes come from pain, a question can occasionally become an answer, and a season of silence, when God is on mute, can somehow speak to us and through us, loud and clear.'[6]

To close this section, here are a couple of psalm-like prayers written by pupils:

'Dear God, sometimes I wonder if things will never look good because the world has things like cancer.
Why do you let that happen to our kind?
I'm just confused, that's all God.
Please take this into account even though I don't believe in you.'

'I know I don't follow you and I'm angry at you,
but if you're there, please help my parents,
help my nan get better, and give a sign that you're there.
I feel alone and I hate it.
I don't want to be alone anymore.'

Asking Big Questions

Lat Blaylock is the editor of *REtoday* magazine in the UK and he is an exceptional communicator – he's able to bring the topics of faith and spirituality to life like very few other people I know. Most teenagers say they don't like Religious Education, but I'm convinced that if they had Lat as their teacher, it would be one of their favourite lessons. He's also been a good friend and advisor to Prayer Spaces in Schools for many years, so we invited him to speak at one of our annual conferences in Leeds.

'One of the things I love the most about prayer spaces,' he said at the start of his keynote talk, 'is the space they give pupils to ask questions. Questions are an important part of our faith journey – they are important for us, and they were important for Jesus too.' He then asked the conference participants a question: 'How many questions do you think Jesus asked in the gospel narratives?' After a few guesses, all of which fell a long way short of the correct answer, Lat said, 'It's 307! The gospel writers record Jesus asking 307 questions. So let's have a look at some of them, shall we?'

On the screen behind him, a list of Jesus' questions began to scroll, and every now and again Lat read one out:

'But if the salt loses its saltiness, how can it be made salty again?'[7]

'Why do you look at the speck of sawdust in your brother's eye and pay no attention to the plank in your own eye?'[8]

'Why are you so afraid?'[9]

'Are your hearts hardened?'[10]

'Do you see this woman?'[10]

'Who do you say I am?'[12]

'Don't you believe that I am in the Father, and that the Father is in me?'[13]

'Simon son of John, do you love me?'[14]

And so on. When the list finally ended, Lat pointed out that although Jesus asked a lot of questions, he rarely answered the questions that other people asked him. And even when he did, he often answered with another question! 'Isn't it interesting,' Lat commented with a slightly mischievous smile, 'that Jesus' preferred teaching method seems to have been to ask questions, rather than telling people things. Whereas our – the Church's – preferred teaching method seems to be to *answer* questions that people aren't even asking!'

What's Your Big Question?

My favourite prayer activity is one that we simply call Big Questions. You can find the details at the end of this chapter, but it basically invites pupils to imagine that God is sitting at the table with them (whether they believe in God or not), and then it asks, 'If you could ask God one question right now, what would it be?' Pupils are usually invited to write their questions on torn-up cardboard (as you can probably tell by now, most of the prayer spaces I run involve a lot of torn-up cardboard) or pieces of paper, which they peg onto string hanging from a gazebo frame. This way, pupils can read one another's questions, and this often leads to some great conversations.

Pupils write all sorts of big questions for God. Here are a handful of examples from prayer spaces that I've helped to run:

- *'How did you ever think of names for things?'*
- *'Are we really alive?'*
- *'Why is there only one of you?'*
- *'Could we live on Mars?'*
- *'You allow wars. Why? ☹ = War ☺ = No War'*
- *'Does everyone go to heaven?'*
- *'Why did you make wasps and flies?'*
- *'Wat was the first crisps called?'*
- *'How can God listen to everyone's prayers all at once?'*

Some questions, as you can probably see, are 'head' questions. They're 'How?' and 'What?' and 'When?' questions, to do with knowledge and theory (and sometimes theology). However, most of the questions in prayer spaces are 'heart' questions. They're 'Why?' questions, and more specifically, 'Why did this happen?' questions.

When I was a teenager, the big apologetic question – the big faith question – was to do with how the universe came into existence, and it was summarised as Creation v. Evolution. It was a head question – a question of knowledge – and I heard talks about it, I read books about it, and I had plenty of conversations with friends at school about it. But in fifteen years of hosting prayer spaces in schools, and having read thousands of pupils' big questions, I can't remember seeing a single one relating to the Creation v. Evolution debate. But what I have seen are hundreds of variations on another apologetic question, which is: 'How can there be a God of love when there is so much suffering?' At first, this also sounds like a head question – that is, 'I don't understand how an all-powerful God of love wouldn't intervene in suffering.' However, even when it is disguised as a head question, pupils are usually asking it as a heart question – that is, 'Does God care about *my* suffering?'

I think that this is one of the big apologetic questions of our time – 'Does God care?' – and it needs a response if children and young people are going to begin a journey of faith. They (and we all, if we're being honest) need to know, first and foremost, that God hears us and God cares for us. And this question, 'Does God care?' is uniquely answered, of course, in Jesus. In him, we discover a God who listens, who cares, who receives people (even the unlikely ones, those unwanted by others) and he includes them. In Jesus, we discover a God who crosses every barrier and boundary in order to reach out and touch lives.

When I'm explaining the Big Questions activity, I sometimes mention that even Jesus prayed a question prayer, one that wasn't answered in the way that he hoped. In the Garden of Gethsemane, Jesus knew that the path ahead involved terrible suffering and violence, and so he prayed, 'My Father, if it is possible, may this cup be taken from me.'[15] There isn't a question mark at the end of this sentence, but Jesus is clearly asking his Father a profoundly human question: 'Is there another way?' There wasn't another way, of course, because this was all part of God's great salvation plan, and so Jesus continued his prayer with the incredible words, 'Yet not as I will, but as you will.'[16]

It seems to me that something important was happening at that moment. In Eugene Peterson's paraphrased version of Jesus' teaching on prayer in Matthew chapter 6, he writes, 'When you come before God . . . just be there as simply and honestly as you can manage. The focus will shift from you to God, and you will begin to sense his grace.'[17] As Jesus' focus shifted from the terrible suffering and violence that he could foresee to his Father's great salvation plan, I wonder if this was a unique moment in which he sensed and received God's grace. It is a tough truth that God doesn't always give us the answers we want to hear or receive, but it is an incredible truth that God does promise to always give grace. God always gives himself.

Prayer spaces offer pupils opportunities to ask big questions about their own lives and relationships, about things that are going on in the world, and about God and faith. Children and young people don't always receive the answers they want to these questions, but the act of asking is important. And asking questions is good education too. For example, the national non-statutory guidance for RE in the UK states that it should 'provoke challenging questions about the meaning and purpose of life, beliefs, the self, issues of right and wrong, and what it means to be human'.[18] (Although I haven't researched this, I would be interested to know if education systems in other nations also encourage asking questions.)

And asking questions is also the way of discipleship. Questions are the paving stones of faith. Our spiritual journeys, according to author and theologian Henri Nouwen, require 'the creation of space in which the validity of the questions does not depend on the availability of answers but on the question's capacity to open us to new perspectives and horizons'.[19] Questions were, as we read earlier, Jesus' preferred teaching/discipling method, so we should encourage them. We certainly shouldn't be afraid of them, and we should resist the temptation to answer questions too quickly – those being asked by children and young people, as well as our own. As one prayer space volunteer said to me, 'Some of these questions for God are really tricky . . . I'm glad I don't have to answer them!'

Encountering God (aka Miracles?)

Emma and I have three daughters, all now grown up, and the middle one has been profoundly deaf since she was born. When she was two and a half years old, she endured a long operation at Great Ormond Street Hospital to receive her first cochlear implant, and when it was switched on a few weeks later, she heard sounds for the very first time. It was a magical moment, but it was also the start of a very long journey for her, and for us too.

Around that time, Emma and I were at a day conference for parents with deaf children, and the main speaker was an American therapist who specialised in deaf communication. None of the parents in the room were deaf, but as he spoke, every now and again he would start using sign language as well as spoken words. Each time it happened, he'd laugh and apologise and return to his talk, but before too long he'd start signing again. After the third or fourth time, everyone else was laughing along. 'I'm sorry,' he said, smiling, 'but I often feel like I can express myself better with signs than I can with spoken words.

'Let me give you an example,' he said. 'There are at least two ways to sign the words "I know", and they mean very different things. Here's the first sign for "I know".' He touched the side of his forehead with the tips of his fingers together, a bit like a military salute. 'And now here's the second sign for "I know".' Keeping his fingers together, he poked them into his belly, just below his ribs. 'Both of these signs mean "I know" – they're both kinds of knowing – but they're very different. Would anyone like to have a go at guessing the difference?' Hands immediately went up around the room because the answer was obvious. The first sign meant head knowledge, information, mental comprehension, cognition, knowing *about* something. The second sign was something deeper. It suggested intuition, inspiration, knowing from experience, having a gut feeling about something. It occurred to me later that no one in the room knew (cognitively, in their heads) the American signs that the speaker was using, but we all still knew (in that we sensed, we intuited) what the signs meant.

Just to help you visualise this (and just for fun!), I've

included a couple of photos of me doing the two signs. I'm sure you can figure out which is which, just like we could.

Sometimes we know (deeply feel) things long before we know (cognitively understand) them. I think this is exactly what happens in prayer spaces in schools every single week. Pupils use the simple, creative prayer activities and afterwards many of them describe sensing or experiencing things that they can't fully explain. They know (deeply feel) that something has happened, even though they don't yet know (cognitively understand) what it is. More often than not, as I listen to children and young people describe what they've sensed or experienced while using the prayer activities, it seems clear to me that they've encountered the presence of Jesus . . . they just don't know (cognitively understand) it yet.

Miracle? Coincidence?

The Prayer Spaces in Schools team regularly posts photos of prayer activities and feedback from pupils and staff on social media. Back when we were using the social media platform called Twitter, we received the following message/tweet:

> Hi!Thanks to you all for your amazing ideas. Pupil has had a bad skin rash (allergies) for 2wks. He walked in with a rash . . . prayed on a (1/2)

It ended abruptly because at that time Twitter limited the number of characters in each message to 140, and we had to wait a couple of minutes for the second half of this exciting message to arrive. When it did, we were astonished:

> Post it for it to go as it made him feel sad . . . he left with no rash!
> Miracle? Coincidence? But he's a very happy boy. ☺
> (2/2)

I've researched and fact-checked every story for this book, because I really want you to feel as confident as I do in what you're reading. When I contacted the teacher who sent us these messages, this is word for word what she replied:

> Hi! Yes, I'm doing well, thank you. Wow – he's in high school now and I'm now a Deputy Head teacher at another school. So much has happened since then but I didn't forget any of it! This 9 year old boy had a rash on his legs that had been bothering him for a while. The parents had tried the normal antihistamines, etc. and the GP had prescribed creams but they hadn't worked. He was self conscious of the rash at the time. We were having a special 'prayer space week' and the boy was in a group of 8 writing prayers onto sticky notes and adding them to the bubble lamp – he clearly

> wanted his rash to go away. By the time we left the prayer space (less than an hour later) it had gone! We brought up his Mum (who was volunteering in the lower school) and she was shocked, but also delighted! We all felt it was a miracle, and I remember the Mum saying to her son, 'See what happens when we pray!' My heart broke!

No one prayed for this nine-year-old boy while he was in the prayer space. And no one told him what to write on his sticky note either. He wrote what he wanted to write, and something impossible happened as a result – they 'felt it was a miracle'. Did they know (cognitively understand) it? Perhaps. Did they know (deeply feel, experience) something? Absolutely.

Faithless Prayers

During my second or third prayer space, I was standing beside the door of the classroom when a thirteen-year-old girl hobbled in on crutches. I offered her a chair, which she refused, and instead she stood beside me while Marcus finished introducing the prayer space to the rest of her classmates. When he was done, I asked the girl if she'd like me to help her to join in with the others who were exploring the prayer activities, but she shook her head. She clearly had no idea what was going on, and it seemed like she didn't want to know either. We had plenty of people on our prayer space team that day, so I decided to stay and chat with her and her two friends.

She told me that a horse had trodden on her foot the previous week, breaking one of the metatarsal bones. (Apparently, soccer players and ballet dancers often break these particular bones . . . as well as those who get trodden on by horses.) 'Does it hurt right now?' I asked, to which she grimaced and replied, 'Yes, a lot.' When she said that she was worried about how long it was going to take to heal, I heard myself replying, 'You know we're Christians, right? Well, there are loads of stories in the Bible about Jesus healing people, and most Christians believe that Jesus still heals people today. Maybe I could say a little prayer about your foot? What do you think?' The girl, and her two friends, stared at me as if I was from another planet. 'Er,' she said, 'I don't know.'

I didn't know what they thought about church or Christians or Jesus or prayer, but my guess was they just thought it was all a bit weird, so I tried to think of something that might make it all seem just a little less weird. 'Praying doesn't have to sound religious,' I began. 'It could just be something like this . . . Dear God, you know about this broken metatarsal, and you know the pain that it's causing. Could you please fix it? It would be great if you did, partly because it's hurting, but also because then she would know that you're really interested in her life. Thanks. Amen.' I didn't close my eyes or change my tone of voice. I just 'talked' the prayer, as unweirdly as I could. The girl frowned, and then her curiosity got the better of her. 'OK,' she said, smiling, 'if that's all it is, yes, you can pray.' I laughed, 'Well, I kinda just did,' and they laughed too. And to be completely honest with you, I was happy with that. These three friends had met a Christian who was a normal person (relatively speaking) and they'd heard a prayer that wasn't too weird, and who knows, maybe they'd give it a go themselves sometime. I quietly prayed that these seeds would go into good soil.

That was Thursday, and the prayer space ended the next day. The following Monday afternoon I was in a meeting, so I couldn't answer my phone when Michelle, my PE teacher friend, called, but she left a voicemail for me. 'Was it you who prayed for the girl in the prayer space last week?' the message began. 'Because she had no pain in her foot over the weekend, and so her parents took her back to the hospital for another scan this morning. She came into school this afternoon, without her crutches. I just saw her. She bounced up to me saying, "I don't have a fracture any more! I think it was a miracle!"'

Daily Miracles

We have to be careful when telling stories like these. To be really honest with you, I wasn't even sure whether to include them in this little book or not. Don't get me wrong, I love to hear miracle stories like these because they encourage my faith, and they remind me that Jesus is alive and doing incredible things, in and through his body, the Church. However, I sometimes worry that these kinds of stories can also become distracting. When we focus too much on skin that has been suddenly made smooth and bones that have been inexplicably repaired, these can become the only kinds of signs and wonders that we seek, and therefore the only ones we see, and we miss the multitude of 'smaller' miracles that Jesus is doing every single day.[20] I wonder if this is part of the reason why Jesus occasionally told the people he healed to keep quiet about it.[21]

Feet aren't getting fixed every week in prayer spaces, and skin rashes aren't disappearing every week either. But miracles are taking place nonetheless, and maybe some of these are the really breathtaking, tear-jerking, life-changing ones. The young person who emerges from the Be Yourself tent with a big smile on her face, standing just a little taller – that's a miracle. The child who writes, 'It was really fun – God spoke to me!' on the feedback sheet – that's a miracle. The young person who says, 'I felt something inside me when I did that activity – I don't know what it was, but it felt good' – that's a miracle. And the child who writes, 'I felt all warm and tingly when I tore up my sorry and put it in the bin' – that's definitely a miracle. The child who writes, 'For the first time, I feel peace' – that's a miracle. And it is too for the one who writes, 'I believed in God before, but now I've been in here I believe in God a bit more.' These are all miracles, and they're each a drop in a vast ocean of miracles that have taken place in prayer spaces in schools all over the world. Children and young people have encountered God and experienced God's reconciliation in all sorts of ways – they may not fully know (cognitively understand) what they've experienced yet, but they know (deeply feel) that something special has happened, and they're often eager to talk about it.

The Greatest Miracle

'I can't do this because I don't believe in God,' said an eight-year-old girl in a primary school in Leeds. 'That's OK,' said Rach, one of the volunteers, 'you don't have to participate if you don't want to.' 'I want to, but my mum says that we're atheists,' replied the girl. One of the other volunteers showed the girl around the activities and explained that she didn't have to pray in order to use the activities. Gradually the girl began to join in. She wrote a wish for people suffering in the wake of the tsunami in Japan, and added her sticky note to those already completely obscuring Japan on the world map.

And then, at the Big Questions activity, she wrote, 'Are you there God, because I just don't know?' Finally, she wrote her name on the big In God's Hands activity, which felt significant. A simple step of personal faith.

And perhaps this is the greatest miracle of all – that children and young people feel welcomed, just as they are. They experience something of God's generous, hospitable heart when they enter a prayer space and meet the people hosting it. They feel like they belong, even though many of them don't yet believe. 'Let the children come to me,' says Jesus, continually. We're doing our best, Jesus.

Prayer spaces awaken something that is already within the soul, within the spirit of every child and young person (and parent, and staff member, and classroom cleaner who also happens to visit them), whether they realise it or not, and that 'something' is a deep desire to be reconciled with God, to belong, to be known and loved by the One who made them. It's the deepest longing in every human heart. Every other longing is but a pale reflection, a weak echo of this one deep longing. The longing to belong.

Reflect and Pray

1. It's OK to not be OK. Is there an area of your life where you feel 'not OK' at the moment? Is there something that you have avoided talking with God about because you feel too hurt, too angry, too confused? Maybe it's time to speak.

2. Flick back to the pupils' big questions that I listed . . . Which of these is also yours? (Hopefully not the one about crisps!) Or maybe yours isn't on that list? If you could ask God one question right now, what would it be?

3. Think about children and young people you know. Who really needs a miracle right now – any kind of miracle?

PRAYER ACTIVITY: BIG QUESTIONS

As I said earlier, Big Questions is my favourite prayer activity, so I just had to include it in the book.

What is it?

We all have big questions about life, about God and faith, and so on. This activity invites pupils to ask their big questions as prayers. Some of them are head questions, things we find difficult to grasp and understand. But most of them are heart questions, to do with our experience of pain and suffering, doubt and disappointment, and so on.

How does it work?

You can set up this activity in all sorts of ways. As you've read, I prefer to hang pieces of string from a gazebo and then invite pupils to write their big questions on torn-up cardboard and peg them onto the strings. This allows pupils to read each other's questions and discuss them, if they want to. You could just as easily (but perhaps less effectively) do this activity with a whiteboard, or with a large sheet of paper on the floor, or with chalks on a pavement.

Who is it for?

This activity works well with children of all ages. And I mean *all* ages – seven-year-olds and seventy-year-olds alike. In fact, perhaps we 'older' children would do well to be as honest as younger children about our big questions?

Any other information?

This prayer activity works best when someone from your prayer space team is available to encourage the pupils to ask honest questions. Sometimes, pupils might want to talk to them about their big question. If this happens, it's really important that the team member answers honestly, even if it's to say, 'I really don't know.' In fact, the best response is often, 'That's a great question. What do you think?' The focus of this activity is on the asking more than on the answering. The purpose is to reinforce the idea that questions are OK. In fact, asking honest questions is essential to authentic faith.

Instructions

Everyone has big questions about life. What are your big questions? Whether you believe in God or not, if you could ask God one question right now, what would you ask?

A little story . . .

Instead of a story, I thought you might like a few more big questions that pupils have written – there are some crackers in this little lot:

'Why are there different religions?'
'If God is real, why did he let my Grandad die?'

'Why don't we always feel you God?'
'Why don't you reply?'
'How is Jesus getting on?'
'Are you Morgan Freeman?'
'Are we in a simulation?'
'Do you love me?'
'Why is the ice cream machine always broken?'
'Why do people have bad rabbits?' (It's possible that I've read this wrong. Maybe they meant 'habits'.)

Part 3

An Invitation . . . Come On!

How are you doing so far? I hope that you feel *inspired* by the stories you've heard – stories of children and young people whose lives have been transformed in hundreds of tiny ways by things that they've experienced in prayer spaces in their schools. And I also hope that you feel *informed* by what you've read in the last few chapters about reconciliation.

This final part of the book is the shortest. I've included a little bit of what we've learned about how to create great prayer resources for children and young people, and then it's the really important bit – it's the invitation for you to join in. Come on!

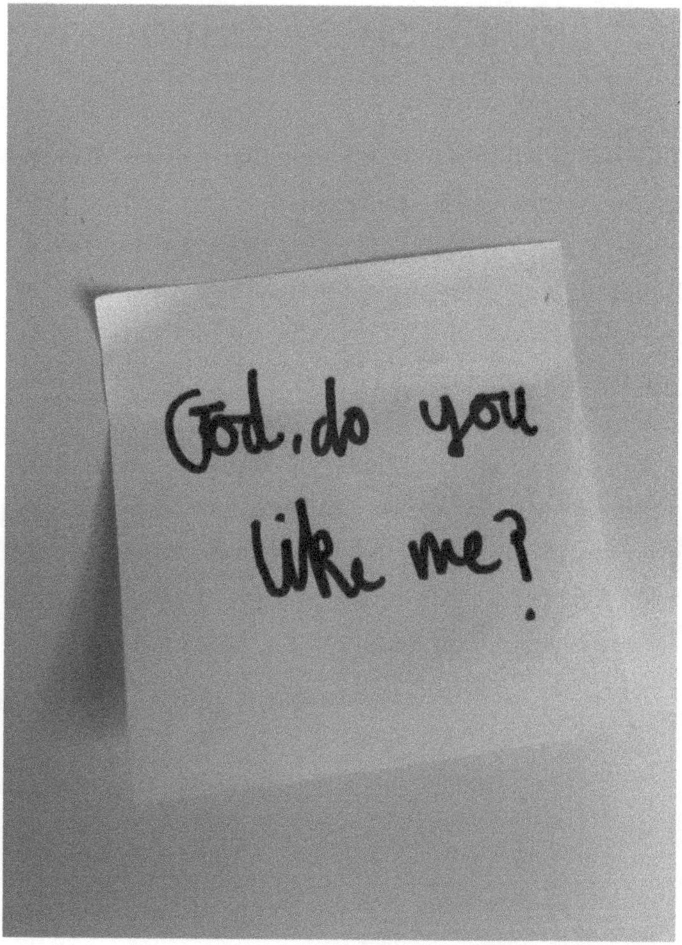
God, do you
like me?

9

How to Create Great Prayer Activities

. . . and how to avoid creating rubbish ones

What pupils say: '*I think these activities have really made me look more into considering religion. I feel like I should maybe try speaking to God at some point.*'—Boy, aged fifteen

What charity leaders say: '*What we're doing with prayer spaces is creating a language which anybody at any age can use, and that's why I think prayer spaces as a model is so compelling and so important.*'—Tim, (former) National Director, Scripture Union UK

* * *

Throughout this book, I've described lots of different prayer activities.[1] After tracking and supporting more than 7000 prayer spaces in all sorts of schools – church schools and state schools, primary and secondary schools in more than thirty-five nations around the world – we've learned a few things about how to create great prayer activities, and how to avoid creating really rubbish ones. We've noticed that the prayer activities that work really well seem to have some things in common, and that's what this short chapter is all about.

I usually deliver the content from this chapter as an in-person workshop, and when I do, the session always begins with a fun exercise. First, I ask the workshop participants to get into groups of three or four, and then I invite each group to pick one random object out of a bag as it gets passed around the room. The objects really are random – I usually grab a couple of things from various rooms in my house, or if I've got a bit of a budget, I go on a shopping spree up and down the aisles of the nearest pound shop/ dollar store and pick the first twenty objects that catch my attention . . . a pair of socks, a plastic tiara, a pack of cards, a toilet brush, a bouncy ball, a keyring, a photo frame, a dog's lead, and so on. The more random the better.

Then the groups are given five minutes to come up with a prayer activity using the object they've picked. I let them decide if it's going to be used by children or young people, but the activity must make good use of the object. When the five minutes are up, I ask each group to present their new prayer activity to the rest of the workshop participants, and then we all give them a round of applause (whether it's good or not). Sometimes, groups come up with some amazing prayer activities, and a few of them have since been used in prayer spaces.

(If you've got a bit of time, why not have a go at the exercise? Have a look around wherever you are right now, and grab the first object that catches your attention. Now try to come up with a great prayer activity using that object. If that felt too easy, choose a different object and try the exercise again. Please let us know if you come up with any brilliant ideas.)

After having a go, the groups usually realise that while it's possible to turn almost anything into a prayer activity, not all of them turn out to be good ones. And so I go through the following guidelines for creating the best possible prayer activities, and each of the eight points begins with a question.

1. Is it simple?

Is your prayer activity simple? Does it have one clear focus? And can you explain it in one sentence, without using any abstract concepts or religious words? If so, this is a great place to start – you're definitely on the right track. Remember the words of Jesus, 'With a God like this loving you, you can pray *very simply*'[2] (emphasis added).

Good examples of simple prayer activities would be The Empty Chair and Calm Jar. (Remember that snow globe you had when you were a child? That's what a calm jar is. You can even download a recipe for what to fill it with from our website.) A less-good example of a simple prayer activity would be one I saw called Idols. The instructions invited pupils to shape some playdough/plasticine into something that was really, really important to them. Then the pupils were asked to crush what they'd made as a way of saying to God that they didn't want whatever it represented to take God's place in their lives (as though it were an idol).

There are a number of reasons why this activity is problematic, the main one being that it isn't simple. It's possible that a few of the pupils may have come across the word 'idol' (or 'idolatry') in the Bible, and if so, I wonder what they would've made with the playdough, knowing that idols are bad things? Most pupils, however, would probably read the word 'idol' as a positive thing – that is, someone to emulate, to admire, to be like. So, what if a pupil made a playdough model of their mum or their dad, which they were then asked to squash again? What does this say to them about God? I think you can see why this isn't simple.

2. *Is it real? Is it relevant?*

Jesus told stories about farmers and fishermen because he was talking with farmers and fishermen. He talked with the crowds about their own lives, using examples and telling stories that they could relate to. In doing so, he helped them to connect with God from the vantage point of their own lives. This is important. When creating prayer activities, don't start with a Bible story or a religious concept. Start with what's going on in the lives of children and young people. What are they excited about, worried about, struggling with, confused by, angry or sad about? Your prayer activity needs to begin with something – a theme, an experience – that all the children or young people can relate to.

Good examples of relevant prayer activities would be Big Questions and Weightlifting Worries. A less-good example would be one I saw called The Armour Of God. On the table was a large Bible open at Ephesians chapter 6, the bit where Paul encourages his readers to 'Put on the full armour of God, so that you can take your stand against the devil's schemes.'[3] Beside the Bible there was a plastic sword, and aside from a sheet of paper with the title of the activity, there was nothing else. Nothing explaining the Bible passage (and I do think it needs explaining), and nothing about what to do with the plastic sword. I would be very surprised if any of the pupils felt that this prayer activity was relevant to them. And you won't be surprised, I'm sure, to hear that most of the children (especially the boys) simply whacked each other with the plastic sword!

3. Is it creative? Is it interactive?

As we've already acknowledged, prayer is more than words. In fact, our words sometimes get in the way of simple, honest communication with God. Searching for the right words to pray with can somehow lead us away from expressing what's really going on inside us.

'Prayer,' writes Dave Tomlinson,

> 'is one of the most democratic activities I can think of. No one owns prayer. No one can dictate how prayer should be offered, or by whom. Anyone can pray: anywhere, anytime, and in any fashion they choose. There is no right or wrong way to do it, no required formula of words. Words may not even figure. Prayer doesn't have to be said in a church (or a mosque or a synagogue), or with any special functionary present. It is soul talk – the voice of our deepest, truest self, aired through whatever language or gesture we choose.'[4]

'Soul talk' – I really like that. Prayer is anything that enables my soul to speak. So, what helps you to express your deepest, truest self? Dancing? Singing? Writing poetry? Playing music? Drawing or painting? Running? Making things (or destroying them)?

It's important that your prayer activities are creative and interactive; that they involve something to do. It's OK to use words sometimes, but it's good to include a mix of wordy and non-wordy activities. The best prayer activities involve something to reflect on and something to do as a response, such as tear this, drop that, write this, move that, tie this, wipe that, make this, walk over there, etc. If it's fun or exciting, even better. A good example of an interactive prayer activity would be Forgiveness Stones. Another would be Bubble Wrap Prayers, which simply invites pupils to imagine 'giv[ing] all their worries and cares to God'[5] as they pop the bubbles on the plastic wrap.

4. Is it welcoming and hospitable?

Wherever Jesus went, he reached out and welcomed people – he demonstrated the hospitality of God to everyone he met, regardless of their wealth, their occupation, their nationality, or even what they believed about him. Jesus still reaches out to people like this, and as his followers, so should we. In fact, we Christians should be the most radically hospitable people on the planet.

One of the questions I often get asked is whether our prayer spaces are 'multi-faith' spaces, and my response is usually something like, 'If you mean, are our prayer spaces similar to typical "multi-faith" prayer rooms that include specific images, instructions and items that are examples of the way that people from different religions pray, then the answer is no, they're not, and so no they're not "multi-faith". However, if you mean, is everyone welcome, then the answer is yes, absolutely! Our prayer spaces are open and hospitable to everyone – those who have a faith, as well as those who don't – and we are confident that the prayer activities will be real and relevant to everyone who participates.' Personally, I'd prefer to simply say that our prayer spaces are for all human beings, full stop – behind the labels (given and received), we're all made of the same stuff, and we're all hungry and thirsty for reconciliation in all of the ways that we've been exploring in this book.

A prayer activity (and prayer itself) can sometimes be challenging, but it should never exclude people, and so it's important to ask yourself: is this prayer activity I've created hospitable and welcoming? And not just towards children and young people from different faith backgrounds, but also towards children with different learning styles, academic abilities, personality types, and so on.

Good examples of welcoming prayer activities would be ones that every pupil can relate to, like Reconciliation Zips and Stress Less (which invites pupils to let go of negative stress in their lives). A less-good example would be one I saw called Pray For Your Non-Christian Friends.

I liked the simplicity and the creativity of it – pupils were invited to write a friend's name on a piece of paper, roll it up and push it into a small bottle, like a message in a bottle. However, even though this was in a church school, it's unlikely that every pupil would've described themselves as a Christian, and those who didn't may have felt a bit unwelcome when they found that at least one of the activities wasn't for them – it was *about* them! On this occasion, I encouraged the prayer space team to simply rewrite the title without the 'Non-Christian' bit.

5. Is it takeawayable? (Is it sticky?)

OK, I know that takeawayable isn't a real word, but you know what I mean. Will the children and young people be able to repeat your prayer activities in their own time and space? Will they learn things as well as experience things? A simple way to make sure they are takeawayable is to create prayer activities using items that they will have at home, or will encounter in their everyday lives.

Ten-year-old Ellie lives in Northern Ireland and she is an outstanding five-kilometre runner. While on a training run one day with her parents, she suddenly stopped running, veered off the path and headed down some steps onto a beach. There she walked to the water's edge and bent down to grab some handfuls of sand. After holding them for a few seconds, she let the grains slowly trickle through her fingers. Her parents were understandably puzzled and when they asked what she was doing, Ellie explained that she was feeling anxious and worried about some things and she suddenly realised that she wanted to let them go. 'I learned this at a prayer space in my school,' she said. 'I just wanted to feel lighter.' The extraordinary thing about this story is that the prayer space had taken place two years earlier.

When schools closed as a result of the Covid-19 pandemic we designed a few Covid-themed prayer activities for families to use at home and then we put them on a PDF. The PDF was downloaded tens of thousands of times over the next few months, so we decided to adapt more of our activities into a 'Prayer Spaces at Home' format. You can download any and all of these from our websites. Good examples of takeawayable prayer activities would be Prayer Wall – we've heard lots of stories of children and young people turning the back of their bedroom door into their own prayer wall – and Mountain: Climbing Shoes (see below for details).

6. Is it personal, and is it communal too?

Do your prayer activities provide opportunities for personal reflection and solitude, and also for dialogue and companionship with others? As Jesus demonstrated, there are times and circumstances when we need to go alone in prayer,[6] and other times when we need our friends to go with us.[7] Most of the prayer activities are personal, so I'll just mention a couple of the communal ones. Good examples would be Character Cards and Thankful Ducks, both of which involve reflecting and talking with someone else.

7. Is it Jesus-like?

I couldn't think of a better way to phrase this question, but what I mean is this: are you clear about how your prayer activities reflect the words, the works and/or the way of Jesus?

Prayer activities don't all need Bible verses attached to them, but it is nevertheless important that we know why we're doing what we're doing. It's a good question to ask whenever you create a new prayer activity: how does this reflect the words, the works and/or the way of Jesus?

I'm confident that I could choose anything from our online resource libraries as good examples of Jesus-like prayer activities. I'll pick a couple of my favourites though: Pray For The World, because God so loved that world that he sent Jesus,[8] and Be The Light, because Jesus calls us to be the light of the world.[9]

8. Is it two-way?

According to the Gospels, Jesus' disciples only asked him to teach them one thing: how to pray. It's possible, of course, that the disciples asked Jesus to teach them loads of things – I definitely would've asked Jesus to teach me how to multiply one packed lunch into enough to feed thousands, or maybe that walking-on-water thing – but even if they did, the gospel writers decided that only one thing was worth recording: 'Teach us to pray.'[10]

The disciples were familiar with prayer, of course. As Jews, they probably would've prayed three times a day, so why did they ask Jesus to teach them how to pray? Was it the confidence and authority that Jesus prayed with? Was it the effectiveness of his prayers – that is, that things actually happened when he prayed? Or was it the intimacy of Jesus' relationship with his Father, and the way he listened for and heard his Father's voice, that the disciples saw and wanted to learn for themselves? My guess is that it was all of these (and possibly other things too), but I have a feeling that Jesus' intimacy with his Father was top of the list.

When Emma and I took our middle daughter along to the Speech Language and Hearing Centre (SLHC) in central London for a hearing assessment, we honestly didn't have high hopes. She was around four years old at the time, and it was two years since she'd received her first cochlear implant during an operation at Great Ormond Street Hospital. After months of calibrating and tuning, the cochlear implant had been turned on, and we knew that she was hearing sounds, but she wasn't developing anything resembling speech. We'd been warned not to expect too much, so maybe our lack of hope was a bit of self-preservation. But then a good friend recommended the SLHC, so we scheduled an appointment.

While we sat talking with the centre's manager, a trained speech and language therapist (SLT) was playing with our daughter on the floor beside us. After a while, we stopped talking to simply watch, and to our surprise our daughter was trying to copy the sounds and mouth shapes that the SLT was making. The manager smiled at us and said, 'From what I've seen over the last thirty minutes, your daughter is clearly capable of learning to speak. She can hear, but what she needs to do now is learn how to listen.' She could hear things – people talking, cars driving past, birds singing, music playing – but she didn't know what any of these sounds were, and so she needed to learn how to listen.

I wonder if that's what Jesus' disciples felt like? I definitely feel like I need to learn how to listen for the voice of God among all the noise in my life.

Prayer is meant to be two-way communication. It is an incredible gift that we can speak to God. Perhaps it is an even greater gift that God speaks to us, and so we need to learn how to listen. When you create new prayer activities, ask yourself: do they provide opportunities for children and young people to pause, to be still and listen for God's voice? (And also, what will you do when God speaks?) A good example of a two-way/listening prayer activity is Letters From God. Another is Forest Listening, which simply invites pupils to pay attention to sounds outside, and to reflect on how they feel about what they can hear.

The Most Basic Task

The great Catholic writer Henri Nouwen once wrote, 'I am afraid that in a few decades the Church will be accused of having failed in its most basic task: to offer men [*sic*] creative ways to communicate with the source of human life.'[11]

If Nouwen is right (and I think he is), then our *most basic* task – the most important thing we can do (and the thing that we will be admonished for if we don't do it) – is to help people to pray: to commune, to connect, to meet with God for themselves. Our primary task is to host and hold spaces of encounter, and to offer simple, creative ways/tools to help people to enter and experience the presence of God more easily, whether they realise that's what's happening or not. I believe that's what these prayer activities can do, and it's what prayer spaces are for – and over the last fifteen years, hundreds of thousands of children and young people have used them to try praying, many for the first time in their lives.

Reflect and Pray

1. If you skipped doing the activity at the start of this chapter, give it a go now. Find an object and see if you can come up with a great prayer activity using it.

2. Have a look at the 'Prayer Spaces at Home' activities in our online resource libraries and download one to try this weekend with your household, whoever that includes.

3. When did you last make space and time to listen to God? What did God say? When and how are you going to make space and time to listen next?

PRAYER ACTIVITY: MOUNTAIN: CLIMBING SHOES

We originally designed this prayer activity for pupils and their families to use at home, during the Covid-19 pandemic, but it's been downloaded from our online resource library thousands of times since.

What is it?

Life is an adventure, full of opportunities and challenges. This activity is part of a series called 'Mountain', and it helps children and young people to reflect on the challenges in their lives that feel as big as a mountain. Perhaps they're anxious about exams, or struggling with a relationship in school or at home, or maybe someone they love is facing a health challenge. These challenges can feel difficult to overcome. Sometimes the real challenge is that they feel like they are facing it alone.

How does it work?

For this activity, all you need is a pair of outdoor shoes and some steps or stairs.

Who is it for?

People of any age can do this activity. (Bear in mind though that it may not be accessible for people with particular disabilities.)

Instructions

When we face personal challenges it can sometimes feel like we're climbing a mountain. It's hard work and it may feel like it's never going to end. What challenges are you facing today? You need to wear good climbing shoes if you want to take on the challenge of climbing a mountain. Put your outdoor shoes on and slowly climb up some steps or stairs. As you do this, think about the challenges in your life, and if you want to, ask God to give you strength.

A little story . . .

Instead of me telling you another little story, why don't you put this book down for a few minutes and go and try this activity for yourself? What challenges are you facing right now? If you want to, talk with God about how you're feeling right now, and ask God for what you need to keep going.

I think
this place
could change
somones
life!

10

Just Getting Started

What pupils say: *'I don't even believe in all that stuff, but I could feel God in there!'*—Boy, aged sixteen

What teachers say: '*I have not experienced anything like the effect of this project before in my career – it was a privilege to work with all those involved and a deeply humbling experience.*'—Head of RE, UK

The First Conference

Looking nervously at the roomful of faces in front of me, I tapped the microphone to check if it was working and repeated my well-rehearsed words, 'Welcome to the first Prayer Spaces in Schools Conference!'

This was back in October 2011, and it had been four years since the first four prayer spaces in schools had been created. The prayer space I'd helped to host at my daughter's school had been one of twelve the following year, and that's when things really started to accelerate. The next year, we tracked and supported forty-eight prayer spaces in schools, and the year after that, there were more than a hundred.

For the day conference, we'd booked the beautiful basement at St James's Church, Clerkenwell, in London and we'd publicised it by emailing the information to our tiny database of interested people and by popping an open invitation onto the 24–7 Prayer website. We expected about forty people to show up, but by 10 a.m. I'd already counted 100, and a few people were still trickling in. Across the back of the hall we'd strung a washing line and then written the names and dates of every school prayer space that we knew about onto revision cards and pegged them along it. The cards filled the line, from one end to the other, and people added more throughout the day.

'Where are you all from?' I asked as I looked around the hall. 'How many of you have experienced a 24–7 Prayer Room in your church?' I expected most people to put their hands up, so I was shocked when only about twenty-five of the hundred or so did. We thought that the conference would be full of people who'd hosted 24–7 Prayer Rooms and who now wanted to learn how to take the principles of creative, hospitable prayer and reflection into schools. Yet here we were with a roomful of people who'd not even done anything like this in their churches. We didn't know what had brought these people to our conference, but they seemed hungry to find out more. It was exciting. It felt like this thing was going to grow, but back then we had no idea just how much.

Bridge to Nowhere?

Chris Curtis, the director of Youthscape, one of the most innovative youth organisations in the UK,[1] was our keynote speaker that day. After telling a couple of stories, Chris projected an aerial photograph of a bridge onto the wall behind him. 'This is the Choluteca Bridge in Honduras,' he began, 'and as you can see, it's quite unique.'

The Choluteca Bridge was originally built in the 1930s as an essential connection between two regions. Over the years, though, the bridge had been damaged by the violent storms that plague the region, and so the Honduras government decided to rebuild it. They recruited the brightest architectural minds and some of the best engineers in the world, and the new, improved Choluteca Bridge was finally reopened in 1996.

Just two years later, the bridge faced its crucial test. Hurricane Mitch, an enormous Category 5 storm, battered Honduras and much of the Caribbean, damaging buildings and destroying dozens of bridges.

All except the Choluteca Bridge, that is, which stood its ground and survived, seemingly unscathed. Nonetheless, there was one big problem, and it could be clearly seen on Chris's aerial photo. The strength of the storm had completely diverted the course of the river. Instead of flowing beneath the bridge, the river had carved a new path, sweeping away one of the roads leading up to the bridge. Despite its state-of-the-art design and its world-class construction, the Choluteca Bridge was no longer fit for its intended purpose.

'The questions we need to ask are simple ones, but they have big implications,' Chris said. 'Are the ministries, the projects, the events that we've built still fit for purpose? Do they still do what we intend them to do? Or have crises come and has the culture changed around us while our attention has remained on what we've been building instead?'

Chris concluded by drawing parallels between this story and Jesus' parable of the wine and the wineskins,[2] but I was still thinking about his questions. Were prayer spaces in schools 'fit for purpose'? Did they really meet the spiritual and pastoral needs of children and young people? Were prayer spaces offering pupils opportunities to experience something of the presence of Jesus, even if they didn't yet realise that's what or who it was? My answer was yes back then – I was convinced that they were fit for purpose, that they did meet these needs and they were making a difference, and as I looked around the hall, I saw a lot of other people who seemed to feel the same. My answer is an even more emphatic yes now.

Prayer Spaces for All

Mordecai's words to his niece, found in the book of Esther, are in my head as I'm typing this because I believe that prayer spaces (in schools, and in other places) are 'for such a time as this'.[3] More than ever before, we need spaces for reflection and prayer – spaces that offer the gift of time and some carefully crafted 'activities that defy acceleration', as we read earlier. Pupils need this, as you've seen from their feedback throughout this little book. 'Too often schools . . . neglect the spiritual needs of their pupils,' said a head teacher after their first experience of a prayer space. 'This is a unique way of redressing that balance.'

School staff need these prayer spaces too, as you saw in the story of my first prayer space, and in Katie's in Kansas City in the USA. Jane Whittington's role with the Church of England's Education Team in Guildford meant that she was responsible for the in-service training (INSET) days for staff, and so she started including prayer activities as part of these days. Jane says that the staff have loved them, even though many aren't Christians.

At a secondary school prayer space in Essex, a pupil beckoned to her RE teacher, saying, 'Miss! You must come and try these prayer activities.' The teacher politely refused, whispering to one of the volunteers, 'I can't even look in here. I'm just going to break down.' Later in the week, the same RE teacher returned and asked if she could use some of the activities after all. Perhaps the most amazing story I've heard is one of the shortest. After visiting a prayer space in her secondary school many times over the course of a week, a teacher realised that she wanted to know Jesus for herself. 'He knocked,' she wrote in an email afterwards, 'and today, at last, I said come in.'

And the parents who visit prayer spaces in schools – even if very briefly – often talk about how they have been affected too. Andy's mum didn't actually visit a prayer space – she was visited *by* one when Adrian brought the Empty Chair activity round to her house. But she laughed and wept as they read the luggage-tag prayers that other pupils had written about her son.

I watched one little girl drag her smartly dressed mum through the door of a prayer space and over to the Fizzy Forgiveness activity. The woman was trying to type something on her phone, but her daughter was already explaining the prayer activity: 'This is where you say sorry for things,' she said. 'What do you need to say sorry for, Mum?' The little girl waited, and the woman sighed and dropped her phone into her handbag. She knelt awkwardly next to her daughter, and as I watched, they dropped their fizzy tablets into the vase together. Over the next ten to fifteen minutes, the two of them did a few other activities, and the woman's phone stayed in her bag. I was standing beside the door as they got ready to leave. The woman looked a bit overwhelmed, so I asked her if she was OK. She paused and smiled, and said, 'I think I've had an epiphany.'

During a parents' evening at a school in the south-east of England, a determined-looking parent approached one of the teachers and asked, 'Are you the one who organised the prayer space?' The teacher braced himself for what he fully expected to be a double-barrelled complaint from this mum, but what he heard was something completely different. She explained that their recent prayer space had helped her fifteen-year-old son to 'deal with some things' and she was intrigued, so she'd visited the school one evening to see the prayer space for herself. 'I spent thirty minutes in there,' she said, 'and it changed my life. I will never forget it.'

The Presence of God

One of the things that sticks in my mind from the very first prayer space that Ruth, James and I hosted is that the comments from pupils and staff changed noticeably over the course of the week. Those who visited at the start of the week generally described what they could *see* – 'It looks amazing in here', 'It looks beautiful', 'It looks like Christmas'. But those who visited for the first time towards the end of the week almost all described how the prayer space *felt* – 'It feels so calm in here', 'Ahh . . . I feel peaceful already', 'Wow, it feels magical', and so on.

If you've been involved with a prayer space in a school or with a 24–7 Prayer Room in a church or in some other place, you've probably experienced this yourself, and I'm sure you've heard comments like these. Something happens – something accumulates – in places where people pray, and the pupils and staff who made the comments above were trying to put it into words. The something that they were trying to describe is, I'm convinced, the tangible presence of God with us, the Holy Spirit. I can't quite get my head around this, but stories in the Bible and events throughout church history and even some of my own experiences convince me that the God who is always everywhere is sometimes somewhere.[4] It makes no logical sense, but sometimes God seems to be more in here than out there, or more out there than in here.

Over the last fifteen years, thousands of school classrooms have become what the early Celtic Christians called 'thin places', places where God seems to be in here (or out there) – somewhere rather than just everywhere. Classrooms and sports halls and tents on school fields have become places of encounter and places of reconciliation. Pupils have learned to love themselves a little bit more – to see and accept themselves as unique and wonderfully made. They've learned to love others, through forgiving and being forgiven. They've learned to love the world in new ways by being better stewards of what God has made, and by engaging with issues of human injustice. And, most importantly, they've felt and received the love of God in small and simple, but potentially life-changing, ways. The children and young people who have experienced reconciliation in these ways may know (deeply feel) that something happened to them while they were in the prayer space, even though they might not yet know (cognitively understand) it. I suspect that they'll be back for more though, that they'll continue seeking in some way, because that's what happens when spiritual hunger is awakened.

- *'The prayer space made me think about prayer and using the sticky notes was really helpful. It gave me a*

way to pray. It was the first time I'd prayed properly.'—Pupil, aged seventeen
- *'It made me think there might possibly be a God.'*—Pupil, aged twelve
- *'I used to believe that God didn't exist but since you lot have come in, I now do.'*—Pupil, aged ten
- *'It was really fun. It made me see God everywhere I look. God has spoken to me.'*—Pupil, aged eight

In spite of everything you've read so far, and everything that's happened in and through prayer spaces in schools so far, it honestly feels like we're only just getting started. A few days before I began writing this chapter, one of my colleagues told me that we'd tracked and supported almost 500 prayer spaces in schools in Great Britain alone this year. I received an email confirming that the first prayer space in a school in the Czech Republic last year has multiplied into twenty-five this year, and I also had a video call with three very excited staff at an international school in South Korea – they'd just hosted their first prayer space (and the first that we're aware of in their nation), and they were already making plans for the next one.

I've got emails in my inbox waiting for me to finish writing this book so I can reply to them, from friends who have recently hosted prayer spaces in schools in Australia, India, France and the USA, and from others who are figuring out how to host them in Canada, Kenya and Albania. In some nations we're also exploring ways to train and resource pupils who want to host prayer spaces in their high schools, which could be huge – and we've got Isi's story to inspire us, which helps. And any time I start thinking that prayer spaces can't possibly work in a particular nation or location, Isi's words give me faith: 'It's weird and sooo cool, since we've done this I think nothing is impossible, and I can do anything with God.'

There's a lot to be glad about and a lot to be grateful for. Prayer spaces are multiplying in schools around the world, and the stories that we hear week in and week out are truly remarkable. God is doing something, that much seems clear to me. And yet, the need is probably greater than ever. 500 prayer spaces in Great Britain last year is definitely something to celebrate. But what about the other 28,500 schools? What about the millions of children and young people in those schools?

I've already included my paraphrase of Eugene Peterson's version of Matthew 9 earlier, but it's worth reading his original version as you consider your response to this book. Let's pause for a moment and think about our school communities – the pupils, the staff, the parents, and others too – as we read these words:

> When [Jesus] looked out over the crowds, his heart broke. So confused and aimless they were, like sheep

> with no shepherd. 'What a huge harvest!' he said to his disciples. 'How few workers! On your knees and pray for harvest hands!'[5]

These words have never been more relevant, because the need for reconciliation in children's and young people's lives – in all the ways that I have described in this book – has never been greater. So confused and aimless they are, like sheep with no shepherd. And yet, so hungry and thirsty they are too. The Spirit of God is at work in this generation, awakening something in children and young people all over the world. Our task is to make it as easy as possible for them to find their way to Jesus. Come on, let's host more prayer spaces!

* * *

At the end of any in-person prayer space training, we usually ask a series of questions to help participants discern the next steps. Maybe they'll help you?

Reflect and Pray

1. **What's in your heart?** How do you feel about what you've read? If you were to choose three words to describe how you feel right now, what would they be? Was there anything – maybe a story or an idea – that particularly inspired you? Was there anything that concerned you?

2. **What's in your head?** What do you think about what you've read? What questions do you still have about how prayer spaces work, particularly in your context? Was there something that I didn't explain well enough? Where could you find some answers?

3. **What's in your hands?** What have you already got that might help you get started (or keep going) with prayer spaces? What opportunities have you got? What relationships have you got? Who do you need to go and talk with about prayer spaces in schools? What resources have you got? What *haven't* you got that you think you'll need? What could you do about this?

4. And I'll add a fourth question, which may be the most important of all. **What do you think God might be saying to you about all this?** Be still and listen.

Notes

Introduction

1. The P.R.A.Y. prayer structure is taken from Pete Greig's book, *How To Pray* (Hodder, 2019) and from 24-7 Prayer's devotional app, Lectio365.
2. Isaiah 6:8.

Chapter 1: The Tale of Four Prayer Spaces

1. Psalm 141:2; Revelation 5:8; 8:3–4.
2. Pete Greig, *Red Moon Rising* (David C Cook, 2015).
3. Marie Stubbs, *Ahead of the Class* (John Murray, 2003).
4. Prayer spaces in schools get called all sorts of things. So far we've heard them called Soul Spaces, Think!, Reflection Spaces, Anam Cara, Sanctum, Quiet Rooms, Stillness Rooms, Orison, Alive! and *Kia Inoi Tātou*, and there are probably many more names out there. The names given to these spaces may differ, but the prayer activities used in them are largely the same. And the stories are always amazing.
5. Gilbert K. Chesterton, *Irish Impressions* (Catholic Way Publishing, 2013).

Chapter 2: Turning the Tide

1. Pete Greig describes God's call on Emma and me to work with 24–7 Prayer, and of God's miraculous provision that enabled us to do so, in his book *Dirty Glory* (Hodder & Stoughton, 2018).
2. Greig, *Red Moon Rising.*
3. To find out more about 24–7 Prayer's network of communities around the world, visit https://www.24–7prayer.com/about/what-we-do/24–7-communities/
4. Matthew 9:36–38, MSG (paraphrased).

Chapter 3: Isi . . . and the Rest of the World

1. Most dictionaries define 'animate' as 'bringing something to life'. Our Maltese friends are the only ones I know who talk about animating prayer spaces rather than organising or running or even hosting them. Bringing prayer spaces to life – I like that.
2. https://sds.mt/spazju-ghal-qalbi/
3. Reuben and the SDS team have even adapted some of the school prayer activities to use during a retreat for couples who were preparing to get married!
4. Acts 28:1.
5 www.prayerspacesinschools.com

Chapter 4: Tea with the Professor

1. Julian Stern and Rachael Shillitoe, *Evaluation of Prayer Spaces in Schools: The Contribution of Prayer Spaces to Spiritual Development* (unpublished, 2017), p. 38.
2. Jack Priestley, cited in Julian Stern, *Loneliness and Solitude in Education: How to Value Individuality and Create an Enstatic School* (Peter Lang, 2014), p. 7.

3. John 3:8.
4. Rebecca Nye, *Children's Spirituality: What It Is and Why It Matters* (Church House, 2009), p. xi.
5. Ibid., p. 6.
6. Ibid., p. xii.
7. Ibid., p. 85.
8. Matthew 5:13–14, MSG.
9. Julian Stern, *Loneliness and Solitude in Education: How to Value Individuality and Create an Enstatic School* (Peter Lang, 2014), p. 169.
10. David Hay with Rebecca Nye, *The Spirit of the Child* (Jessica Kingsley, 2006).
11. Colossians 1:19–20.
12. 2 Corinthians 5:18–20.

Chapter 5: Fearfully and Wonderfully Made

1. Psalm 139:14.
2. https://digital.nhs.uk/data-and-information/publications/statistical/mental-health-of-children-and-young-people-in-england/2021-follow-up-to-the-2017-survey
3. https://www.apa.org/topics/children/mental-health
4. https://www.youngminds.org.uk/media/dp0mu415/pcr144b_social_media_cyberbullying_inquiry_full_report.pdf, p. 5.
5. https://assets.publishing.service.gov.uk/media/5a7acd89ed915d71db8b2946/Child-Wellbeing-Brief.pdf, p. 5.
6. https://www.childrenssociety.org.uk/what-we-do/our-work/well-being
7. https://nces.ed.gov/fastfacts/display.asp?id=1130#fn1
8. Carl Honoré, *In Praise of Slow* (Orion, 2004), p. 275.
9. Lily-Jo, *Talking to Children About Mental Health* (SPCK, 2023), p. 33.

Chapter 6: Let Us Love One Another

1. 1 John 4:7.
2. I've always loved the word 'companion'. As I understand it, the word comes from two Latin words, *com* and *panis*, and so companion literally means 'with bread'. I think of this every time I share the Lord's Supper.
3. Galatians 5:13.
4. Hebrews 10:24.
5. James 5:9.
6. Ephesians 4:2.
7. John 20:23, MSG.
8. Lewis B. Smedes, *Forgive and Forget: Healing the Hurts We Don't Deserve*, 2nd rev. edn (HarperCollins, 2007).
9. https://www.health.harvard.edu/mind-and-mood/the-power-of-forgiveness
10. Matthew 6:9–15.
11. Matthew 18:22.
12. Matthew 5:4.
13. A te reo Māori phrase meaning 'Let's pray!'
14. John 11:33–5.
15. Romans 12:15.
16. https://www.health.harvard.edu/mind-and-mood/the-power-of-forgiveness

Chapter 7: Acting Justly, Loving Mercy, Walking Humbly'

1. Micah 6:8.
2. Lily-Jo, *Talking to Children*, p. 76.
3. Colossians 1:19–10, MSG.
4. 1 Peter 5:7, NLT.
5. Lily-Jo, *Talking to Children*, p. 77.
6. Barna Group, *The Open Generation: United Kingdom* (2023), p. 26.

7. Krish Kandiah, cited in Barna Group, *Open Generation*, p. 29.
8. https://en.wikipedia.org/wiki/Street_children

Chapter 8: Seeking and Finding

1. Matthew 7:7.
2. https://www.churchofengland.org/sites/default/files/2020-01/gs-2161-children-and-youth-ministry-full-with-appendix-final.pdf
3. https://www.barna.com/research/teens-and-jesus/, drawing data from Barna Group, *The Open Generation: United States* (2023).
4. Barna Group, *Open Generation*, p. 26.
5. Psalm 34:8, NIVUK.
6. Pete Greig, *God on Mute*, 2nd edn (David C Cook, 2020), p. 20.
7. Matthew 5:13.
8. Matthew 7:3.
9. Mark 4:40.
10. Mark 8:17.
11. Luke 7:44.
12. Luke 9:20.
13. John 14:10.
14. John 21:16.
15. Matthew 26:29
16. Ibid.
17. Matthew 6:5–6, MSG.
18. https://assets.publishing.service.gov.uk/media/5a7adb3ce5274a34770e7953/DCSF-00114-2010.pdf, p. 7.
19. Henri Nouwen, *Spiritual Direction: Wisdom for the Long Walk of Faith* (SPCK, 2011), p. 9.
20. The opposite is also true, of course. Some Christians seem determined to turn a blind eye to, or to explain away, stories like the ones I've just told.
21. Mark 1:41

Chapter 9: How to Create Great Prayer Activities

1. To find and download all the prayer activities mentioned in this chapter and elsewhere in this book, do an online search for 'prayer spaces in schools' and visit one of our online resource libraries. Everything is free!
2. Matthew 6:9, MSG.
3. Ephesians 6:11.
4. Dave Tomlinson, *How to Be a Bad Christian* (Hodder & Stoughton, 2013), pp. 136–7.
5. 1 Peter 5:7, NLT.
6. Luke 4:1–2; Matthew 14:13; Luke 6:12–13.
7. Mark 14:32–42.
8. John 3:16.
9. Matthew 5:14.
10. Luke 11:1.
11. Henri Nouwen, *The Wounded Healer: Ministry in Contemporary Society* (Darton, Longman & Todd, 1971).

Chapter 10: Just Getting Started

1. To find out more about Youthscape, visit https://www.youthscape.co.uk/
2. Matthew 9:16–17.
3. Esther 4:14.
4. I'm told that the theologically academic terms for this are 'God's omnipresence' and 'God's manifest presence', but I think I prefer the way I described it.
5. Matthew 9:35–8, MSG.